The Reappeared

THE CENTER FOR THE STUDY OF
GENOCIDE, CONFLICT RESOLUTION
& HUMAN RIGHTS

Genocide, Political Violence, Human Rights Series

Edited by Alexander Laban Hinton, Stephen Eric Bronner, and Nela Navarro

Alan W. Clarke, *Rendition to Torture*

Lawrence Davidson, *Cultural Genocide*

Daniel Feierstein, *Genocide as Social Practice: Reorganizing Society under the Nazis and Argentina's Military Juntas*

Alexander Laban Hinton, ed., *Transitional Justice: Global Mechanisms and Local Realities after Genocide and Mass Violence*

Alexander Laban Hinton, Thomas La Pointe, and Douglas Irvin-Erickson, eds., *Hidden Genocides: Power, Knowledge, Memory*

Walter Richmond, *The Circassian Genocide*

Irina Silber, *Everyday Revolutionaries: Gender, Violence, and Disillusionment in Postwar El Salvador*

Samuel Totten and Rafiki Ubaldo, eds., *We Cannot Forget: Interviews with Survivors of the 1994 Genocide in Rwanda*

Ronnie Yimsut, *Facing the Khmer Rouge: A Cambodian Journey*

The Reappeared

Argentine Former Political Prisoners

REBEKAH PARK

RUTGERS UNIVERSITY PRESS

NEW BRUNSWICK, NEW JERSEY, AND LONDON

Library of Congress Cataloging-in-Publication Data

Park, Rebekah

The reappeared : Argentine former political prisoners / Rebekah Park.

pages cm.—(Genocide, political violence, human rights series)

Includes bibliographical references and index.s

ISBN 978–0-8135–6855–3 (hardcover : alk. paper)—ISBN 978–0-8135–6854–6 (pbk. : alk. paper)—ISBN 978–0-8135–6856–0 (e-book)

1. Political prisoners—Argentina—History. 2. State-sponsored terrorism—Argentina—History. 3. Government, Resistance to—Argentina—History—20th century. 4. Argentina—Politics and government—1955–1983. I. Title.

HV9582.P37 2014

365.'4500982—dc23

2013046605

A British Cataloging-in-Publication record for this book is available from the British Library.

Copyright © 2014 by Rebekah Park

Visit our website: http://rutgerspress.rutgers.edu.

Manufactured in the United States of America

For the *Ex-Presos Políticos* of Córdoba, Argentina

CONTENTS

	Acknowledgments	ix
1	"The Battle of the Panties"	1
2	"They Disowned Us Twice"	23
3	Suspicion and Collaboration	44
4	Solidarity and Resistance in Prison	71
5	Life After Prison Still Feels Like Imprisonment	108
6	Post-Transitional Justice	145
	Epilogue	156
	Notes	161
	Glossary	165
	References	169
	List of Former Political Prisoner Interviewees	175
	Index	177

ACKNOWLEDGMENTS

Without the help of many agencies and individuals, this project would not have been possible.

For funding this research, I am deeply grateful to the Jacob K. Javits Fellowship Program, the Pacific Rim Research Program, and the Department of Anthropology at the University of California, Los Angeles (UCLA). The UCLA Center for the Study of Women also provided institutional support and library privileges.

I began working with former political prisoners in Argentina at the urging of Dr. Irene Martínez, a physician, writer, and human rights activist (and herself an *ex-presa política* or "former political prisoner"). Irene introduced me to her *compañeros*, or "comrades"; her fiery spirit and sense of humor continue to be an inspiration. For her wisdom, strength, and mentorship, I thank Sara Liliana Waitman, who, as president of the Asociacion de Ex-Presos Políticos de Córdoba (Association of Former Political Prisoners of Córdoba, or AEPPC) (2008–2011), took me under her wing and became my key informant. Juan Carlos Álvarez, Ester Cabral, Élida "Ely" Eichenberger, Mario Paredes, and Gladys Regalado all provided invaluable support, guidance, and friendship, and answered an endless stream of questions.

None of this would have been possible without the ex-presos themselves. All of the members of the AEPPC welcomed this foreign scholar, sharing *mate* (herbal tea) and their stories. I witnessed their steadfast commitment to social justice. I would like to thank all of the following former political prisoners, the majority of which were formally interviewed: Luis Acosta, Fidel Antonio Alcázar, Juan Carlos Álvarez, Roque José Antonio Anguinetti, María Mercedes "Chicha" Aranguren de Scheurer,

Jorge L. "Caballo" Argañaraz, Américo Aspitia, Atilio Basso, Ester Cabral, Sebastián Cannizzo, Irma Casas, Miguel Carlos "Miguelito" Contreras, Félix "Gato" Cornejo, Cristina Correa, Gloria di Rienzo, Maria Cristina Diaz, Élida "Ely" Eichenberger, Graciela Josephina Feliz, Hugo Luis Fernández, Hugo Roque Ferradans, Víctor Eduardo Ferraro, Ovidio Ramón "Pajarito" Ferreyra, David Lanuscou, Stella Molina, Juan Morales, Silvia Martos, Manuel Nieva, Pedro Nolasco Gaetán, Rosa Noto, Rodolfo "Petiso" Novillo, Mario Paredes, Norma Peralta, María del Carmen "Carmencita" Pérez, Jorge "Villero" Ramírez, Gladys Regalado, Enzo "Gringo" Sacco, Alicia Staps, Carlos Hugo Suárez, Jorge Alfredo Torriglia, Adriana and Alicia Varillas, Viviana "Vivi" Vergara, Juan Villa, Sara Liliana Waitman, and Heldo Zárate.

Carole Browner, Linda Garro, Geoffrey Robinson, Susan Slyomovics, and Jason Throop all provided close readings and critical commentaries, as did two anonymous readers from Rutgers University Press. Carole supported this project from the start, and Susan gave me the language to write about political prisoners, museums, and reparations. Geoffrey and Jason provided very detailed comments on the theory and structure that were instrumental in shaping the final version of this book. Geoffrey helped me realize the most significant findings of my research.

Jena Barchas-Lichtenstein read and offered substantive and stylistic advice and very helpful edits; Hanna Garth, Óscar Gil-García, and Natasha Rivers all read versions of individual chapters. I also thank Marilyn Silverman for her meticulous copyediting. I thank Marlie Wasserman for planting the idea to publish my book with Rutgers University Press.

I thank two Argentine scholars, Ludmila da Silva Catela and Jaime Malamud-Goti, as experts on human rights in Argentina. A good portion of this fieldwork was conducted at the Provincial Commission and Archive of Memory of Córdoba, where Ludmila and her staff graciously let me hang around for hours on end.

Muchísimas gracias a los Argentinos Pamela Almada, Natacha González Cendra, Carmen Herrera, Martín Llanos, and Alicia Ester Schiavoni, who all taught me the language and culture in Argentina in the way that only true friends can. Thank you for welcoming me into your homes.

My work with the Córdobese former political prisoners continued even after my return to the United States through Alicia Partnoy and Ana Deutsch; their quick reception and warmth were greatly appreciated, as well as their scholarly insights on their own personal experiences. I would like to thank Ram Natajaran, Eva Roekel, and Katja Seidel for being wonderful compañeros to collaborate with, and exchange ideas on Argentina's human rights scene.

Cricket Buchler, Abby Fifer-Mandell, Lauren Gutterman, David Lowenfeld, Sally Mendelsohn, Jeff Park, Barbara Sheen, Suzanne Wertheim, and Kristin Yarris generously gave me personal and moral support.

Finally, I must thank Jonah Lowenfeld, Ezekiel Agustín Lowenfeld, and Zooey Corina Lowenfeld. Everything in my life is better because of Jonah, and my children, who both sat patiently in my womb during the writing of this book.

The Reappeared

1

"The Battle of the Panties"

Argentina's history of state terror is infamous: during the most recent military dictatorship, which lasted from 1976 to 1983, thirty thousand political dissidents were kidnapped, tortured, and "disappeared"[1] in secret concentration camps. The victims became known as *desaparecidos* (the disappeared). In response to the fact that their children were sucked up[2]—as if the earth had opened up and swallowed the person whole—desperate families, who faced dead ends or death threats from state authorities, formed human rights organizations in search for their missing children. It took until 2005, for trials against former military officials to resume after a period of impunity, and these families' persistent demands for justice have made Argentina a world leader in human rights, focusing attention on the violation of forced disappearances. Since the return to constitutional rule in 1983, Argentina sought to recover from its disgraceful legacy of human rights abuses through a variety of means, including not only through the formation of a truth commission, but also through ongoing trials, monetary reparations, and memorials. Although Argentines do not use this term,[3] this recovery process is known in English as transitional justice.

Many scholars have written about this "Dirty War"—as the military juntas labeled it—and about human rights more generally in Argentina (Guest 1990; Brysk 1994; Abregú 2000; Vezzetti 2002; Robben 2005), as well as about the transitional justice efforts (Acuña and Smulovitz 1995; Jelin and Kaufman 2000; Ageitos 2002; Feld 2002; Novarro and Palermo

2003; Payne 2003; Grandin 2005; Sikkink 2011). So much has been written about this era in Argentina, that some scholars refer to the family-based human rights groups and their activism around dictatorial crimes as part of the "old human rights advocacy organizations" (Humphrey and Valverde 2008). Karen Ann Faulk's book, *In the Wake of Neoliberalism: Citizenship and Human Rights in Argentina* (2012), centers on the shift of focus in human rights concerns in Argentina from torture and forced disappearance, to impunity and corruption as the most pressing violations in the past two decades, and focuses on the new protest movements that reflect this trend. With members of the *Madres de Plaza de Mayo* (Mothers of Plaza de Mayo, or *Madres*) and the *Abuelas de Plaza de Mayo* (Grandmothers of Plaza de Mayo, or *Abuelas*), the brave mothers and grandmothers who searched for their disappeared children and stolen grandchildren, beginning to pass away, and with the literature on this era already vast, scholars have turned to Argentina's "new" social protest movements around issues of security, migrant labor rights, and police brutality (Dinerstein 2002; Garay 2007; Betrisey 2012).

But the final word has not been written about this period and about its aftermath. Despite the Argentine human rights activists' ocean of efforts to remember the past or to keep the past in the present, very little scholarship and public attention have addressed *ex–presos políticos* (former political prisoners), many of whom were first disappeared into torture camps and then made to reappear in legalized prisons (Merenson and Garaño 2010). Most scholarship on this period deals instead with the struggles of family-based human rights groups (Bouvard 1994; Arditti 1999; Da Silva Catela 2001). Although scholars frequently included survivor accounts in their broader work, they focused almost entirely on survivors' torture experiences (Daleo 1998; Feitlowitz 1998; Taylor 2001), and not on their roles in the transitional justice process as both recipients of symbolic and monetary reparations, and as active participants. There is even less written on the development of organized groups of political prisoners in the mid-2000s, and its relation to the perceived failure of transitional justice in addressing the needs of survivors. The emergence of this movement of former political prisoners reveals another important shift within the Argentine human rights movement, but one that still revolves around violations committed during the dictatorship, and that therefore has gone largely unnoticed. But this shift is fundamental to acquiring a more complete view of the diversity within the human rights movement in Argentina, one that casts a different light on the effectiveness of transitional justice efforts thus far.

The topic of political prisoners is contentious within the human rights community and among Argentine citizens because of accusations or suspicions that they must have done something to have survived, or that they had committed extreme violence by supporting armed revolutionary movements that ultimately failed to take over the country. In the past decade, collectives of political prisoners have published edited volumes on their time in prison, in large part—as they mention in their introductions—because they believe that their memories attest to an important part of Argentina's history that might otherwise be forgotten or unknown (Asociación Civil El Periscopio 2003; Berguan 2006; Sillato 2008; Asociación de Ex Presos Políticos de Córdoba 2009). In reaction to these testimonial texts, scholars and journalists have debated the moral justification for guerrilla activity and the presumed guilt of the survivors (Guelar, Jarach, and Ruiz 2002; Oberti and Pittaluga 2006). These debates included such questions as whether militants should have been armed or not, and whether former militants are overidealizing the past and avoiding sensitive topics surrounding their survival (Gelman and La Madrid 1997; Marchak 1999; Lorenz 2002; Bonaldi 2003; Longoni 2007).

This book is about the formation of the AEPPC, the first group of political prisoners that was recognized by the state as an official organization with its registered legal status, at a particular time in Argentine history and at a particular point in their lives. I sought to understand their views on early transitional justice efforts and why they demanded more. The AEPPC's formation has everything to do with the past, present, and future of transitional justice in Argentina. This book challenges the notion that survivors have been fully acknowledged—as is often assumed—and questions who qualifies as a victim in this particular case of transitional justice.

A New Organization

This is the first study conducted on an organized group of self-identified former political prisoners in Argentina. AEPPC members described themselves as both victims of state terrorism and as survivors of torture camps, prisons, and state repression. That the AEPPC members consciously call themselves ex–presos políticos, is significant because they feel that this label reminds the public of the political reasons behind their imprisonment, a fact that they believe the terms *sobrevivientes* (survivors) and *ex-desaparecidos* (ex-disappeared) do not engender.

Based on twenty-one months of fieldwork in Argentina in 2006, 2008, and 2009, most of it spent in Córdoba with the AEPPC, this book explains why political prisoners lacked visibility in the early development of the family-based human rights groups, as well as why they later demanded more financial reparations than the ones they received in the 1990s. The AEPPC was organized in February 2007, when it obtained *personería jurídica* (legal status); however, the members began meeting informally in 2003, and the group was previously known as the Commission of Former Political Prisoners. They do not represent all of the survivors in Argentina, or in Córdoba Province, but they reflect an important dissenting voice that broadens our views of human rights and of the purpose of memorials. The AEPPC invited me to work with them in Córdoba. I stayed until I had reached a certain saturation point, when the data began repeating itself, and for as long as I could emotionally immerse myself into the violent past.

AEPPC membership includes those who were imprisoned for political reasons in Argentina during the 1970s and 1980s. At the time of the interviews, the AEPPC members lived in Córdoba Province and were between the ages of fifty-three and seventy-five. All of the AEPPC members identified themselves as activists, primarily in labor unions, but also as artists, intellectuals, and progressive Catholics. Their level of formal education ranged from primary school to university or they held technical degrees, though all were well informed on Marxist theory, national liberation movements, and labor history.

At the start, political prisoners in Córdoba organized in response to health and economic problems they and fellow former cellmates faced post-release, which increased as they aged. "No one was looking after our needs, so we had to form our own organization," said Sara Liliana Waitman, the AEPPC's first president (Waitman, September 2008). While it is well-known that torture survivors suffer aftereffects over the duration of their lives, the forty-five political prisoners I spent time with, thirty-nine of which I formally interviewed, allege that they had been silenced for decades, because of the stigma surrounding them. They needed a new organization, particularly one based outside of Buenos Aires, because they found themselves without a place in the human rights movement, despite being the direct witnesses of what happened in the camps and in the prisons.

The trajectory of these political prisoners—their marginalization and eventual recognition as victims of state terrorism—demonstrates that while the human rights paradigm was presented as an apolitical alternative to the failed utopic revolutions to achieve social justice (Moyn 2010), human rights can be, and are used, as a political strategy to assert broader moral agendas. The participation of political prisoners in the human rights movement and the latter's acceptance of former guerrillas, demonstrates that the meaning of the term *human rights* has changed over time in Argentina, as have the actors. It is not simply that the AEPPC has conformed to the new era, in which human rights is the currency for social change, but that the family-based human rights groups have also become more politicized over time. This change provided the context in which political prisoners could emerge as activists within the Argentine human rights movement. Though this movement is often presented as unified, the tension between political prisoners and the families of the desaparecidos is essential to understanding the political prisoners' experiences in post-dictatorship Argentina.

In short, this book disabuses us of the notion that human rights can be used to protect all victimized groups at all times, or put in another way, that there exists one type of victim and that all of the victims receive the same levels of support. Who got defined as the quintessential victim in the post-dictatorship era, and the types of violations that counted for purposes of reparation, have everything to do with the ex-presos' struggles to gain recognition as survivors of state terrorism and their demand for symbolic and economic reparations. Ex-presos want a place in memorial museums and pensions for the suffering induced by the legacies of state terrorism.

From this research, I conclude that a post–transitional justice era, a period that applies to countries like Argentina which have already experienced an initial transition period but have not yet overcome the violent past and its aftermath, offers us another chance to remedy human rights abuses.

To understand why political prisoners have formed organizations and demand more reparations, it is necessary to gain a better sense of who they are, and to understand what happened to them during the 1970s and 1980s. I begin with the story of María Cristina Díaz, who was imprisoned for belonging to her school's student council, and whose political views were predominantly shaped by her upbringing. Cristina's case illustrates how ten thousand people became political prisoners, the fear they faced in prison, and the ongoing repression they faced upon their release.

Generations of State Violence

Shortly before Cristina was born in 1952, her father, Florencio, moved from San Nicolás, a small town in Buenos Aires Province, to the country's central province of Córdoba to find work. Back then, Córdoba was the center of industrial production in Argentina. Thousands of workers labored in the city's car-manufacturing plants. Florencio worked at Fiat, eventually becoming a supervisor, until he suffered a serious factory accident. A loose screw from a piece of machinery flew into his face, fracturing most of his facial bones. With extensive surgery, he regained sight in one eye, but lost a considerable amount of skin. Still, Florencio went on to become a union leader within the Fiat factory.

Florencio's labor activism was an outgrowth of his family's political affiliation with Peronism, the political ideology and politicking associated with one of Argentina's most famous political leaders, Gen. Juan Domingo Perón. Perón's first two terms lasted from 1946 to 1955, after which he was forced into political exile and the Peronist Party was outlawed. He was a charismatic populist leader who succeeded in gaining supporters from the left and from the right. His second wife, Eva Perón, was adored by the masses for her dedication to workers, women, and children, and she became a popular icon for equality among left-wing activists. Perón and his wife instituted extensive social reforms that benefited the poor and the working class, including providing public hospitals and playgrounds for children.

Florencio was involved in unionizing during one of the most important events in the history of Córdoba Province and of Argentina as a whole: the 1969 "Cordobazo." By coordinating their efforts for the first time, university students at the National University of Córdoba and automobile factory workers joined together in protest and immobilized the city of Córdoba for several days, helping to bring down the dictatorship of Gen. Juan Carlos Onganía, who had led a coup d'état in 1966. This was the first university established in Argentina and its students were known for their radicalism. The Cordobazo sparked similar movements throughout the country, and this event came to define Córdoba as the center of revolutionary and intellectual movements—an identity that the city retains even today.

With protests taking place all over the country, Onganía resigned and Gen. Roberto M. Levingston continued the military-led "Argentine Revolution," which opposed both liberal democracy and communism. It was during Levingston's nine-month rule that the federal police detained Florencio for his labor union activities and for his involvement with the leftist Peronist movement. He was soon released, but because he feared being detained again, he and his family immediately went underground. That state violence against political opponents was commonplace even before the start of the dictatorship in 1976 reveals that a system of repression was already in place; the torture and forced disappearances were simply at the extreme end of the spectrum.

Since Argentina's independence from Spain in 1816, a common pattern developed in the transfer of power between democratically elected presidents and military rule. Political opposition parties were frequently outlawed. And as repression increased throughout these periods of military rule—which included targeted killings, forced political exile, bans on particular political parties, and expulsions of intellectuals from universities—armed resistance groups formed in opposition. By 1970, several students and labor union members joined two guerrilla groups: the Montoneros, the left wing of Peronismo; and the Ejército Revolucionario del Pueblo (People's Revolutionary Army, or ERP), the armed branch of the Partido Revolucionario de los Trabajadores (Workers' Revolutionary Party, or PRT). Other parties and movements, including the Communist Party, also existed, but the Montoneros and the ERP had captured the dreams of a liberated Latin America among most of the Córdobese former political prisoners.

Unemployed after living underground, Florencio bought a small store in 1972, to make a living. However, the front door of his business was bombed immediately after he did so and the family, as a result, lived in constant fear. Although he was a committed factory worker, Florencio encouraged his daughter, Cristina, to excel in school. Cristina made a half-hearted attempt, but abandoned her studies for factory work instead. Bent over a machine all day, however, Cristina soon regretted dropping out. And so, at the age of nineteen, she told her father that she wanted to return to primary school. Despite being surrounded by twelve-year-olds, Cristina enjoyed being a non-traditional student and eventually joined the student council.

After Onganía and Levingston, the third de facto president, Alejandro Lanusse, appointed Héctor Cámpora as his succeeding presidential candidate. Cámpora, however, left after just two months in office. Before stepping down, Cámpora appointed Raúl Alberto Lastiri to oversee the transition and granted a full amnesty (Law 20508) to all of the political prisoners who had been held during the 1966–1973 military rule. Those imprisoned were primarily students, banned political party members, and trade unionists. Argentina returned to electoral democratic rule when the citizens elected Perón, who came out of exile in Spain, where he had been since 1955, to assume the presidency for the third time in 1973.

During the time Cristina was in high school, between 1973 and 1975, both the right-wing and left-wing factions of the Peronist Party had grown in size. They had also grown apart from each other during Perón's exile. When Perón returned to Argentina on June 20, 1973, his left-wing supporters gathered to greet him at Ezieza International Airport. Snipers who belonged to the right-wing faction, and whose presence Perón himself had approved, shot at the crowd, killing 13 people and injuring 365 more. The celebratory mood surrounding Perón's return was brief, though, as he died only a year later in 1974. His third wife, María Estela "Isabel" Martínez de Perón, assumed office, but everyone considered her ill-equipped due to her lack of previous political experience. She allowed the head of the ultra-right-wing *Alianza Anticomunista Argentina* (Argentine Anti-Communist Alliance, or Triple A), José López Rega, who was also the minister of social welfare, to take control. Under Isabel's brief tenure, the Triple A continued to assassinate leftist political opponents, mostly workers and students, in secret "pilot" concentration camps. The dictatorship would later increase the number and usage of these kinds of torture camps. Between approximately 600 and 2,000 people were killed during Isabel's short presidency, and 425 of those killings are directly linked to the Triple A (Robben 2005, 138). In reaction, guerrilla leftist groups adopted a more confrontational strategy that included targeted assassinations and amateur bombs, which contributed to the general chaos that now consumed Argentina.

Amid protests and growing unrest at inflation, unemployment, and political violence, the military took over the government in 1976, allegedly to bring order. It was known as the "Gentleman's Coup," so unremarkable was it for Argentina to have another coup d'état. This coup was led by Lt. Gen. Jorge Rafael Videla, Adm. Emilio Eduardo Massera, and Brig. Gen. Orlando Ramón Agosti. The military junta leaders justified their actions by stating that they were fighting Communist terrorists. However, even at the height of the movement in 1974–1975, there were no more than 2,000 guerrillas, and only 400 of them had access to arms (Feitlowitz 1998, 6). Leaders of the revolutionary groups fled the country, and as a result, all of the guerrilla groups were dismantled. Rank-and-file members who remained in the country lost their support networks and went into hiding—some lived in internal exile throughout the dictatorship, while others were kidnapped. Since many military juntas had come and gone in the past, there was no serious opposition when the military stepped in as Isabel failed to govern. In previous dictatorships, those who opposed the government were often imprisoned but were eventually released. This military dictatorship, however, was different.

The dictatorship suspended the constitution and enacted what it called the *Proceso de Reorganizacion Nacional* (Statute of the Process for National Reorganization, or *El Proceso*, the Process), which aimed to transform Argentina into a Christian, "civilized," and Western nation through the control of all judicial, legislative, and executive powers. Leftists, intellectuals, and others were labeled as threats to national security, and anyone suspected of being a "subversive" or someone who prevented this Process, was disappeared.

In February 1976, one month before the coup d'état, Cristina's father was put in the local *cárcel común* (regular prison) in Córdoba, *Unidad*

Penitenciaria 1 de San Martín (Penitentiary Unit Number 1 of San Martín, or UP1). His Peronist affiliation and syndicate leadership position were enough to make him a target. A month earlier, after the disappearance of twenty-four people in Córdoba, family members of disappeared victims had begun meeting as a group, the *Comisión de Familiares de Detenidos Políticas* (Commission of Families of Political Detainees). To avoid being taken down with her father and disappeared herself, Cristina switched schools and managed to graduate in June 1976. A month later, a group of civilians[4] working with the military, went searching for Cristina at her mother's house. Because Cristina was living elsewhere, they went after her brother instead. In an attempt to force him to divulge his sister's location, the group of men beat and tortured him. But neither her brother nor her mother knew where Cristina lived; Cristina purposely never told anyone her location to protect her family. The same group of civilians went looking for Cristina again on July 8, 1976.

As the dictatorship mandated that Argentina's Independence (July 9) be observed at school, Cristina attended her school's celebration. Her brother, knowing Cristina was forced to attend, appeared at the school's party to warn her that some men were looking for her. Cristina said to her brother, "Let's leave separately. And if something happens—if they detain me or kidnap me—immediately file a legal complaint; submit an appeal for asylum for me" (Díaz, December 2008). Newly informed of the state's ongoing surveillance of her, Cristina departed again, this time to live with her partner and extended family in an attempt to protect her immediate family members. She continued to move around for about two years to escape the military. Around the time that Cristina went into hiding, in September 1976, the *Familiares de Desaparecidos y Detenidos por Razones Políticas* (Families of Those Disappeared and Imprisoned for Political Reasons, or *Familiares*) established themselves as an official organization in Buenos Aires, with branches as well in other provinces, one of which was the first group of family members to have come together in Córdoba.[5]

Meanwhile, Cristina's mother was devastated by her husband's imprisonment and feared losing her daughter as well. In October 1976, the military removed her husband Florencio from UP1 and executed him. Cristina's mother, who was uninvolved in politics, had trouble understanding the events around her. At that point, Cristina was now living with her aunt and uncle to prevent the military from finding her.

On April 30, 1977, a group of fourteen mothers began holding demonstrations in the plaza in front of the presidential house, *Casa Rosada* (Presidential Palace), in response to reports of torture and the continued disappearance of their children. This group became the Madres, the first to openly protest the dictatorship. Later, hundreds of other mothers would join them in the march, both in the capital and in the main plazas of interior provinces. In 1977, other mothers, the Abuelas, also began searching for their missing grandchildren, who had been stolen from disappeared female prisoners. Many pregnant prisoners had been forced to give birth in captivity, separated from their newborns, and eventually killed. These babies were given away to torturers and to military sympathizers.

A year after the Madres and Abuelas officially organized, Cristina returned home and hid for two months, never stepping outside. She eventually became restless and said to her mother, "Look, everything is fine; I'm going to go out and find a job" (Díaz, December 2008). Cristina found work that same day. Two months later, in September 1978, when she came home in pain after having her wisdom teeth removed, she found her home completely surrounded by a large group of men on all sides, including the roof. She recognized one of the men as her neighbor who lived around the corner. The men took Cristina to Mariano Moreno, a street in the center of the city of Córdoba, where one of the police intelligence offices— *Departamento de Informaciónes de la Policía de la Provincia de Córdoba* (Center of Police Intelligence of Córdoba Province, or D2)[6]—was located.

When the *grupos de tareas* (lit. "task groups," but understood as "death squads") detained prisoners in Córdoba, more often than not, they took them to D2, where they beat and tortured them during interrogation sessions before deciding where to send them afterward. Some were transferred to one of the *campos de concentración* (concentration camps), such as La Perla or La Ribera; in other cases, they were sent to a regular prison, such as UP1. Prisoners at the concentration camps were considered to have disappeared because there was no official record that these places even existed, or that persons were even missing. Captives were often handcuffed and blindfolded, thrown into a car trunk, taken to a hidden location, and then tortured during interrogation sessions. In concentration camps, prisoners remained blindfolded the entire time. Some of these prisoners survived, but most died, and others were transferred to other camps or prisons. Regular prisons, particularly at the start of the dictatorship, were not necessarily safer than the concentration camps, as some prisoners were executed and all were regularly tortured, either physically or psychologically. When prisoners arrived at UP1, the military did not inform their families, and all forms of legal representation were denied.

The military held Cristina, blindfolded and handcuffed, at D2 for twenty days. From D2, the military transferred Cristina to UP1, where her father had been held and executed two years earlier. At UP1, Cristina was placed in the fourteenth block, where the political prisoners were held, apart from the *presos comunes* (regular prisoners). To increase her sense of isolation, however, Cristina was placed in solitary confinement for three and half months. She had nothing in her cell except a bar of soap, a towel, and a tin can. Twice a day, the guards allowed her to empty her tin can, in which she urinated and defecated. The guards also gave Cristina ten minutes a day to clean herself and her cell. The only interaction she had with others was when the guards dropped off her food.

At the beginning of 1979, the guards took Cristina down to the cells where the other female political prisoners were held. When Cristina entered her cell, other prisoners were taken out and presumably transferred to another prison, though by then a transfer also meant death. After 1976, some women-prisoners were transferred from UP1 to another prison called Villa Devoto in Buenos Aires Province. Others never made it to their next destination. Several former political prisoners who were held in Villa Devoto were later released, since international human rights investigators were allowed to make an inspection.[7]

During her imprisonment, Cristina was brought to trial in front of a military tribunal and was represented by a defense lawyer assigned to her by the dictatorship:

> I don't know why they believed I was secretly linked to the Montone-
> ros. Whatever, they had no proof and I was the only one on trial . . .
> there was nothing to say or to defend, you know, in response to this
> charge they made against me. They took me to trial several times.
> The attorney general gave me twenty-five years but I ended up with

ten years. After the sentencing, they made me stand under a tree for the entire day with two soldiers guarding me. The defense lawyer came up to me a few hours after the sentencing to ask me how I felt and I . . . I don't know if it was out of repulsion or, you know, not really thinking, but I said, "I feel good because I know that I'm not staying in prison for ten years."

"What do you mean that you're not going to be a prisoner for ten years? You were just sentenced."

"Yes," I said, "But you will all be gone before then." Then his face visibly changed. He got nervous and left. (Díaz, December 2008)

Cristina's story of her trial is illustrative of how political prisoners narrate their time in prison with memories of resistance instead of torture and other horrors they endured in prison.

At the time Cristina was imprisoned, there was little understanding of how the military operated and what the fate of any captive would be. Cristina and those in similar situations still faced a tremendous amount of uncertainty, particularly since the dictatorship denied any wrongdoing against Argentine citizens: "Later in the year '79, the OAS [Organization of American States] came and . . . [General] Menéndez denied that we were political prisoners because he said that there were no political prisoners in Córdoba. We had access to the news because we communicated with our families through the regular prisoners. We found out that our families had been mobilizing to get the OAS to come and visit the prison" (Díaz, December 2008).

Cristina was referring to the OAS's Inter-American Commission on Human Rights' on-site visit from September 6 to 20, 1979. In response to the increasing reports of disappearances and torture, the OAS arranged a visit in May 1979. The dictatorship delayed the visit, and spent the four intervening months preparing for the inspections by moving prisoners out of concentration camps and temporarily improving conditions in the regular prisons. Before prisoners spent time alone with OAS officials, the guards threatened them with dire consequences if they spoke the truth.

On April 11, 1980, the OAS released its report based on the investigators' 1979 visits to select prisons, and drew further international attention to the situation in Argentina. Even though the human rights investigators were unable to access all of the secret torture camps, the OAS report was extremely damaging for the dictatorship. Until that point, the military junta leaders denied the existence of any secret prisons, in addition to all reports of torture, executions, and disappearances, and the OAS report uncovered evidence that all of those human rights violations were indeed taking place.

In 1980, Cristina and her fellow prisoners in the fourteenth block were taken from their cells, blindfolded, handcuffed, and driven to an air force base. The prisoners believed that they were about to be released or transferred, but they never left; instead they were returned to UP1 and Cristina remained for another year. This seemingly insignificant trip outside left Cristina psychologically scarred. Whenever prisoners were taken out of prison, they had no way of knowing if they were about to be executed in a so-called shoot-out—premeditated killings that the dictatorship staged to appear as if there had been confrontations with terrorists—headed to a concentration camp to be tortured, or moved to another prison.

The military eventually transferred Cristina to Villa Devoto at a time she remembered was marked by fewer killings—a result of increased international pressure on the dictatorship to account for human rights abuse allegations. When Jimmy Carter became president, political relations changed between the United States and Argentina. According to both declassified documents in the U.S. National Security Archive and the political prisoners, Carter differed from Richard Nixon in both imposing economic restrictions and pressuring the dictatorship to end its practice of disappearances. Political prisoners believe that this change in U.S. policy significantly contributed to ending disappearances and executions, as well as improving some aspects of prison life, such as limited family visits.

Still, Cristina remembered that even at Villa Devoto, the guards kicked and beat the prisoners. Guards committed psychological forms of torture by depriving prisoners of any sense of control, individuality, or dignity. But nonetheless, political prisoners resisted. Cristina recalled the time when she and a group of women-prisoners refused to submit to humiliating body inspections when they first arrived at Villa Devoto—an act of resistance that is affectionately remembered as the *Guerra de las Bombachas* (Battle of the Panties) by the Córdobese political prisoners:

The guards inspected us in an abusive way, and those of us from Córdoba were subjected to one of these searches because of a com-pañera[8] (who had hidden a carmelo[9]). We didn't lower our panties for the inspection; we only stretched them a little and we didn't take off our bras either. But there it was different; you had to take off your panties. We refused to get inspected because we came from Córdoba, from a different way. We said, 'No, not us.' And then they beat us with clubs and said, 'Here, it's yes. Here you have to lower your panties.' (Ibid.).

Julie Taylor also wrote about this event in her article, "Desdemona's Lament," based on her interviews with women-prisoners who had been held in Villa Devoto. In piecing together the story of the asunto bombacha, or "panty incident," Taylor discovered that while this protest expressed the prisoners' commitment to solidarity and resistance, it also produced internal struggles among them. While the prisoners who had belonged to guerrilla groups refused to submit to the bodily searches, other prison-ers without political attachments did not believe it was important to par-ticipate in this act of resistance, because of the risk of losing family visit privileges (Taylor 2001, 110). The AEPPC prisoners who recalled this protest did not speak about the internal division, most likely because the women-prisoners interviewed in this study had activist backgrounds. Córdoba was and still is known for its high level of political activity.

Without concrete evidence to use against Cristina under the Concejo de Guerra (War Council), she was instead set to go before a federal court. One day, after four years in prison, in September 1982, the guards called out her name and she was brought into the main office, where she stood in front of Judge Adolfo Zamboni Ledesma. Cristina remembered that either her mother or a group of human rights activists had managed to secure her a lawyer when she was brought before the judge. At the end of her interview, she accused the judge of being responsible for her father's execution:

His eyes widened and he said, "How am I responsible for the death of your father? Who was your father?"

"My father was Florencio Díaz," I told him. "His trial was held in Tribunal 1 where you presided. A judge should uphold security, but you didn't do this for the life of a detainee. They took my father out of prison and executed him. When I'm released I'm going to bring a case against you." He was completely shocked. Everyone was—the secretary, my lawyer, everyone. (Díaz, December, 2008).

She still expected to be released on December 6, 1982. Cristina's mother traveled by plane from Córdoba to Buenos Aires to reunite with her daughter. But December 7 arrived and Cristina was still in prison. Two days later, believing that they had been tricked by the military, Cristina's mother left money and documents for her daughter with a recently released prisoner, who had been held in the same prison cell as Cristina in Villa Devoto, and returned home.

Soon after her mother departed, Cristina was let out of prison, and she yelled her good-byes to her fellow inmates behind the prison's walls. Nearly all of the women I interviewed remembered shouting out to their compañeras before exiting prison, out of solidarity and to assuage their feelings of guilt over being released while others remained behind. But Cristina was not immediately freed, and was instead forced into a patrol boat with a group of federal police officers:

> They began to threaten me and laughed while they said horrible things. I asked, "On what conditions am I being released? And where are you taking me?"
>
> They replied, "We're going to kill you." And then they put a gun to my head, like in a robbery, and the entire thing was meant to terrorize me. When we arrived at the police headquarters, they took me to a cell.
>
> And I said to them, "What is this? Why am I not being released? Now you're keeping me here?"
>
> They said, "No, we're checking the whole country, province by province, to see if there is any capture order under your name." (Ibid.).

What Cristina experienced immediately before her release was one of the ways in which military officials exerted control over people through fear even outside of the prison. A large number of those released were subjected to constant monitoring under a system called *libertad vigilada* (supervised release, or better understood as house arrest). The military continued to monitor the former political prisoners for months or years, ordering them to live in a particular province, and insisting on regular, mandatory visits to the police.

Cristina was eventually released by the police and left the station with empty pockets. Fortunately, she remembered the address of the other former political prisoner with whom her mother had left money for her to buy a bus ticket back to Córdoba. Traveling home after being liberated felt strange because noisy streets replaced silent prison cells. The currency had changed in value and appearance during the dictatorship, which even made buying a bus ticket an alienating experience. When prisoners returned home, their families had grown older with time and stress. Cristina was nonetheless happily reunited with her mother and brother again.

Reintegration into the broader community, however, was more complicated. In some cases, such as Cristina's, neighbors were both stunned and relieved to see her again after having witnessed her kidnapping. Although bystanders are criticized for their inaction, some neighbors and close acquaintances showed their solidarity by welcoming former political prisoners into their homes and offering them jobs under the table. Others, however, feared being associated with released prisoners, or believed that the prisoners had done something wrong in order to have been taken away by the military. Cristina's story is representative of what was commonly experienced by other AEPPC members. This experience would later lead to a struggle to win both reparations and control over how the past is narrated in Argentina. Cristina waited thirty-four years to seek justice for her father when Federal Court 1 in Córdoba convicted Jorge Rafael Videla and Luciano Benjamín Menéndez, among others, in December 2010, for the torture and murder of thirty-one political prisoners between April and October 1976, at UP1, one of whom was Florencio.

Methodology

Throughout 2006, 2008, and 2009, I conducted participation observation at national memorials and at government buildings in Buenos Aires, and in memorialized spaces, labor union buildings, and homes in Córdoba. During my period of intensive fieldwork in Córdoba in 2008–2009, I spent every day with political prisoners at meetings, cafés, rallies, symposia, lobbying visits, census sites, protests, marches, conferences, social events, and at the first trial against former military officials to take place in Córdoba, in May 2008. I was interested in all of the AEPPC's activities, from their own memory work through film, tours, archival research, writing, and teaching workshops, to lobbying the government for more reparations to supporting trials against former military officials. My intention was to understand what they sought to accomplish through the organization, the internal struggles they experienced in agreeing upon an agenda, and the individual experiences and opinions of AEPPC members. I joined several AEPPC committees to both conduct research and to make myself useful: the editorial team for *Eslabones: Cronicas, Relatos, Poesias, Cuentos, Illustrációnes* (Links: Chronicles, stories, poetry, tales, and pictures), the published volume of testimonies from political prisoners in Córdoba; the production team for the film on UP1;[10] the fundraising team; and the volunteer team whose task was to clean the site of former torture camp La Perla before it was presented to the public. I also served as an informal translator for international visitors for the AEPPC at two different memorialized spaces in Córdoba, and accompanied the AEPPC on lobbying visits with national and provincial legislators.

My work also included spending personal time with individual political prisoners in their homes, parks, academic events, and cafés. Most weekends were spent enjoying *asado*, the traditional Argentine barbecue, or homemade pizza with various political prisoners who generously invited me into their homes. About four times a week, I visited the *Comisión y el Archivo Provincial de la Memoria de Córdoba* (Provincial Commission and Archive of Memory of Córdoba), located in the city's main square at the site of D2, in order to spend time with the AEPPC members who worked there. Although my time there was chiefly spent in observation, I would occasionally help them with archival research, translate tours, and share mate or keep them company during cigarette breaks. During my visits, I would discuss what had happened at the previous weekly AEPPC meeting and learn the latest gossip about the minor disputes that erupted every so often between members.

In addition to my hundreds of informal conversations with political prisoners and with other members of the local human rights community, I conducted thirty-nine oral history archive interviews with AEPPC members, including twenty-two males and seventeen females. The content of these interviews was largely derived from questions submitted anonymously by various AEPPC members. I had collected these questions at their weekly meetings during my first three months in Córdoba. Although four women worked as teachers and one woman as a psychoanalyst, the rest worked in factories or trades, and twenty-four of the former prisoners were in labor unions. Only one AEPPC member had never been imprisoned; however, her husband had died from brain damage he incurred while tortured in a secret detention camp. These interviews focused on members' life histories from birth to their present activism in the AEPPC, and included stories about their militancy, imprisonment, and opinions on justice and reparations. I would also pose additional questions based on previous conversations I had had with that individual about themes that had frequently appeared in my fieldnotes, enabling me to collect quotes on specific topics. Most of the data presented here is drawn from these interviews, which were conducted in Spanish and presented here with my English translations. As requested by the former political prisoners, I have used real names throughout this text except when noted; I used pseudonyms when I was concerned that the party should remain anonymous for speaking on sensitive issues, or when the person wished to remain anonymous.

In order to contextualize the narrated experiences of the political prisoners, I conducted archival research at the *Centro de Estudios Legales y Sociales* (Center of Legal and Social Studies, or CELS) in Buenos Aires, and at the U.S. National Archives in College Park, Maryland. I also collected academic articles from various institutions, libraries, and bookstores on memories, trials, and militancy related to the dictatorship era, and I attended lectures and art exhibits in Córdoba and in Buenos Aires that addressed these topics.

In short, I sought to immerse myself into the world of political prisoners, even renting an apartment from a survivor who spends half the year out of the country. When I lived in the apartment, a photo of her disappeared brother hung on the bedroom wall. I spent every moment trying to grasp why the AEPPC had formed and how they interacted with each other, the public, and with the local human rights community.

The Missing Story of Former Political Prisoners

In conducting this research, I discovered that political prisoners are marginalized in Argentina. They are regarded with suspicion by families of the disappeared simply because they survived, and they are also seen as terrorists by some members of the public. Consequently, political prisoners have served as witnesses in trials against former military officials and helped inform the 1984 truth commission, but they have played a much more limited role as witnesses in the construction of collective memory in the post-dictatorship period. However, in the past decade, as memorialization processes become important political vehicles to pressure the government for more trials, political prisoners have played an increasingly crucial role in developing memorialized spaces, as discussed in chapter 2.

Thus, political prisoners are involved in two memory-making processes in the post-dictatorship era, one is juridical—trials and the truth commission—and the other is political—memorialized spaces. The juridical process limits political prisoners' truth claims with its set parameters of what counts as abuse and when an abuse occurred. Conversely, the memorialization process has enabled political prisoners to speak about "civil death" in Argentina society. For this reason, chapter 3 focuses on the motivations behind the AEPPC's desire to have political prisoners work at memorialized spaces, rather than on their participation in trials and in the 1984 truth commission. The debate over who should memorialize this dark period in Argentina's history and how to publicly commemorate it, is extremely relevant to other societies faced with the task of both remembering and forgetting a violent past.

Throughout my writing on the political prisoners, I have sought to stay close to the concept of agency and to the contradictions surrounding the prisoners' agency. Agency is defined here in the general sense: the ability to act independently in the world, even when authorities and structures limit those choices.[11] More specifically, this concept addresses how the political prisoners acted in prison according to the particular morals prescribed by their political ideologies. They retrieve and share memories that construct identities around their militancy rather than their suffering; in so doing, they become willing agents of their past and present. But if agency is central to their identity, it also deprives them of their victim status.

As agents, they acted and they were punished for their acts. Furthermore, if the political prisoners had agency, the families of the disappeared are left to wonder: What did they do to survive? Conversely, what did they *not* do that could have enabled others to survive? Such questions assume the accuracy of the political prisoners' self-representation as agents. Regardless of its veracity, the balance between agency and responsibility is where the tension lies. While the silent desaparecidos have historically been presented as innocent victims, the political prisoners exclude themselves from that group precisely by claiming agency. But if the political prisoners are deprived of their will (like prisoners in European concentration camps during World War II) and if, as Holocaust survivor Primo Levi, in *The Drowned and the Saved* (1989[1980]) argued, morality becomes gray in the genocidal conditions of a concentration camp, then the political prisoners can become victims. When labeled as victims, though, political prisoners feel that their activism no longer defines them; what defines them instead, is the fact that their captors had tortured them.

It is a commonly-held belief among the AEPPC members that their activist identities helped them survive prison and return to their lives after liberation. Munú Actis, one of the five women-survivors of *Escuela de Mecánica de la Armada* (Navy Mechanics School, or ESMA), a torture camp in Buenos Aires,[12] theorized that some prisoners survived torture and the camps because they had already practiced hiding their real identities before they were disappeared. They had hidden their political activities from their own families to protect them, and even adopted noms de guerre, or "pseudonyms" to avoid other militants from naming them under torture. "Our history as militants evolved gradually. As the repression intensified, our type of militancy forced us to engage in a pretense with others that later helped us to resist inside the ESMA," said Munú (Actis et al. 2006, 27). In chapter 4, I examine how political prisoners expressed *resistencia* (resistance) and *solidaridad* (solidarity) in prison, and now as aging activists. Attempting to retain a sense of their identity as activists, however minor, enabled survival in the past—psychologically and physically—but today, this identity or reclaiming of identity as political activists, deprives survivors of victim status, not legally, but socially.

Yet, the reality is that the political prisoners were dependent on their captors for food, water, space, light, and air. What the political prisoners did, however, was find points of agency amid this repression. In chapter 5, we see the limitations of agency again when the political prisoners were released. They could not control the social and economic conditions to which they returned after their release. Their lives had been irrevocably changed and they spent years attempting to recover what they had lost—and ultimately failing to do so—because they could control neither how others treated them, nor how the bureaucracy in place deprived them of rights given to other victims of the dictatorship. Still, as they seek reparations for what they have suffered, they continue to participate in the creation of memorials and memorialized spaces, and they continue to insist that they resisted both the military and their torturers. By doing so, they pass on memories of themselves as people with agency—however limited.

The final chapter offers the AEPPC member assessments on the transitional justice efforts thus far in meeting their needs. The story of political prisoners in Argentina challenges us to rethink the end goal of transitional justice. It reasserts the productiveness and moral value of remembering the past, and demonstrates the ways in which an emphasis on human rights has both limited and benefited victims of torture and imprisonment. It also makes us rethink what counts as a human rights abuse: for many political prisoners, mourning the loss of what could have been, has been equally or more devastating than the psychological impacts of torture. Lastly, this book offers a victim perspective on transitional justice, which is still rare. This ethnography is of the last group to be heard in post-dictatorship Argentina: the survivors. This is a story of people who were terrorized, marginalized, and repoliticized in the aftermath of one of the darkest dictatorships in Latin America.

2

"They Disowned Us Twice"

Former political prisoners were seen differently at different times. There were periods in which, as survivors of torture camps and prisons, they were regarded as victims worthy of national attention. At other times, as former guerrillas, they were seen as the cause, at least partly, for the violence that took place in Argentina during the 1970s and 1980s. Sometimes, they were even seen as the cause for earlier violence in the late 1960s, when popular resistance movements took the world over. In one period, survivors were seen as powerless victims, and in another, they were seen to be at fault for having been kidnapped and imprisoned. Since the fall of the dictatorship in 1983, various presidents have adopted diverse approaches on dealing with prior human rights abuses. This chapter provides an overview of the transitional justice efforts undertaken thus far, and indicates how the AEPPC members believe that the changing sociopolitical climate over the past three decades impacted popular perceptions of them. The AEPPC members reported that it wasn't until the mid-2000s, that they began to have more control over how they were seen. At that point, there was an opportunity for them to influence public perceptions on their place in history through their participation in memory-related projects. That survivors were not always regarded as victims, led AEPPC members to believe that they were victims twice over: once due to their imprisonment, and a second time due to their having survived it.

This history of transitional justice also intersects with how Argentine human rights groups' early strategies in building support for their cause ended up excluding those survivors who were seen as less than innocent. Even as these same human rights groups expanded their agenda—which splintered the Madres into two different groups[1]—and became increasingly more politicized and more open about the political background of their disappeared family members, the Córdobese political prisoners continued to struggle to integrate themselves into the human rights movement as a result of their early exclusion.

Transitional Justice in Argentina

The transitional justice process began when Argentina returned to constitutional rule in 1983. The dictatorship had lost legitimacy in its spectacular defeat to the British in the war to reclaim the Malvinas—which the British call the Falkland Islands—and when the military prepared for the return to democratic rule by passing a law guaranteeing its members amnesty before holding democratic elections. Raul Alfonsín was elected president and, upon taking office, convened the *Comisión Nacional sobre la Desaparición de Personas* (Argentine National Commission on the Disappeared, or CONADEP) to investigate the fate of the missing people. The CONADEP officially registered 8,963 desaparecidos; its members said that the numbers were in fact much higher, but limited time and resources made it impossible to account for all of the disappearances. In 1986 [1984], the CONADEP published its findings in a report called *Nunca Más: Informe de la Comisión Nacional Sobre la Desaparición de Personas* (Never Again: The Report of the Argentine National Commission on the Disappeared). This document also served as preparation for the historic 1985 Trial of the Junta Leaders, which was televised without sound so as to temper public hostility against the military, and was accompanied by a weekly newspaper that contained the transcripts. Nine high-ranking military officials were sentenced to prison, some for only a few years and others for life.[2]

The trials were set to continue, but several military-led uprisings and the threat of another coup led President Alfonsín to pass two laws that effectively closed the possibility for legal justice: the 1986 *Ley de Punto Final* (Final Stop Law) and the 1987 *Ley de Obediencia Debida* (Due Obedience Law). The first of these laws placed a statute of limitations for filing cases against those responsible for human rights abuses, and the second released lower-ranking military officers from responsibility, under the logic that they were simply following orders. There was, however, one exception to these laws: all those who had a role in stealing female prisoners' babies. During the dictatorship, military families and military supporters illegally adopted approximately five hundred babies who were either born in captivity to female prisoners, or stolen when their parents were kidnapped; those involved in these illegal adoptions were still eligible to be tried.

If the 1985 trial was a success, then the later pardon of all who were sentenced was its undoing. In 1989, Carlos Menem was elected president; in the name of reconciliation, he pardoned those who had already been tried or were about to be brought to trial in 1990. Yet President Menem also granted reparations to families of the disappeared (Law. No. 24.4111) and to those who had been detained arbitrarily (Decree 70/91 Law No. 24.043), which were paid in bonds starting in 1994. But these conciliatory acts did not result in actual societal healing. During Menem's tenure, speaking about the dictatorship became taboo, and state surveillance programs resumed, which meant that people who had been imprisoned for political reasons were monitored and threatened again. It was during this "era of impunity," in 1995, that a new human rights group, HIJOS (*Hijos e Hijas por la Identidad y la Justicia contra el Olvido y el Silencio*, or Children for Identity and Justice and against Forgetting and Silence), emerged in Córdoba and in La Plata. With trials suspended, HIJOS sought to provide an alternative form of justice through "staged protests," or *escraches*, where they publicly shamed individuals responsible for the deaths of desaparecidos. "When there is no justice, there are escraches," is their slogan.

The next ten years brought both upheaval and a return to the transitional justice process. During this decade, human rights groups continued to demand justice and simultaneously to expand their mandates to address a variety of social ills that were seen as a result of growing economic inequalities. After Menem, between 1999 and 2003, there were three presidents in four years, amid serious economic upheaval. Argentina's economy collapsed in 2001, after decades of massive economic mismanagement that began with the dictatorship in 1976, and that continued through Menem's policies of deregulating national industries and accepting large loans from the International Monetary Fund (IMF). Human rights groups, however, continued to pressure the government to resume trials against the military officials, and when the late president Néstor Kirchner took office in 2003, he helped marshal political and judicial support for human rights. He would eventually overturn the Full Stop and Due Obedience laws in 2005, and annul Menem's pardon in 2007. These two events led to the reopening of trials, which are ongoing as this book goes to press. In addition, starting in the mid-2000s, several new memorials and memorialized spaces have been established by the state and are run by human rights groups, in an effort to promote human rights and memory. Kirchner's successor and wife, current president Cristina Fernández de Kirchner, continues to build national policies on human rights through memorials and trials. The transitional justice process is still ongoing, and it has been one of the most influential models for adopting a comprehensive approach to human rights abuses (Arthur 2009).

One of the major impacts of Argentina's transitional justice efforts was the production of official narratives of guilt and innocence that left political prisoners in limbo. These prisoners were seen as simultaneously guilty due to their political actions, and innocent by virtue of being victimized at the hands of the military torturers. *Never Again* and the 1985 trial of the military junta leaders were both premised on what the government called the *Teoría de los Dos Demonios*, or the Two Demons Theory. According to this theory, both the dictatorship and the guerrilla organizations were responsible for the violence that engulfed Argentina between 1976 and 1983, and the rest of society fell victim to both forces (Familiares 2006). Many of the former political prisoners had been part of these guerrilla organizations, and they were now being labeled as terrorists. The Two Demons Theory explained President Alfonsín's decision to try members of the military without undermining the military institution, and to condemn armed revolutionary groups without adding to the suffering of survivors (Perelli 1994, 39–66).

To clarify, the Two Demons Theory did acknowledge that victims existed, but only a certain type of victim. According to this theory, the main group of victims was the general public—the citizens who were caught between the military and guerrilla violence and were silent either by fear or by choice. Those who disappeared were reimagined as innocent youths, and they were also considered victims. During the trial against the junta leaders, which lasted for seven months in 1985, the prosecutors focused on victims who had no political affiliations. "The most powerful cases were presented first, including those victims who had no connection to the guerrilla movements," wrote Kathryn Sikkink, in *The Justice Cascade: How Human Rights Prosecutions Are Chaging World Politics* (2011, 73). Five years after this trial, President Menem would draw on the Two Demons Theory to form the ideological justification for granting a full amnesty to the military's rank and file.

Argentina's transitional justice process unfolded at the same time as human rights emerged as the dominant moral framework in the twentieth century. Human rights gained its strength from being perceived as above politics and as an alternative to armed struggles. In his book, *The Last Utopia*, Samuel Moyn (2010, 141) argues that human rights gained momentum in the wake of the cold war and decolonization movements precisely because the dreams of revolution and popular struggles were deemed failures. Similarly, Bronwyn Anne Leebaw, in "The Irreconcilable Goals of Transitional Justice" (2008, 97) observes: "The spread of transitional justice institutions that investigate past abuses has also been identified as symptomatic of a declining faith in possibilities for collective struggles for political change, and as evidence of a counterrevolutionary agenda." Although many groups later adopted the disappeared victims' politics, the families of the disappeared did not take up the revolutionary cause during the dictatorship, and the desaparecidos were depoliticized. "The disappeared and the imprisoned were presented by their relatives as exemplary children, good students, and members of families living in harmony; in sum, as ideal or 'normal'" (Jelin 2009, 183). Instead, the relatives used human rights—legal and quasi-legal measures—as a strategy to enforce basic legal rights that transcended national borders and politics. By networking with international human rights organizations, family-based human rights groups like the Madres were able to amplify their domestic cause and to more effectively pressure the Argentine government to stop human rights abuses (Keck and Sikkink 1998, 107).

In more recent years, the family-based human rights groups also developed a political critique of the dictatorship's repression. In Córdoba, the former "political prisoners," or *ex-presos*[3] as they call themselves, also adhere to this theory, which considers the dictatorship part of a long-term plan to break apart communal ties. The goal of breaking these ties was to create a culture of individualism, which in turn would pave the way for global capitalism. The military, according to the ex-presos, was a tool for large conglomerates and for the most powerful and wealthy parts of Argentine society—the *oligarquía* (oligarchy)—to implement their economic policies. From the ex-presos' point of view (shared by the members of the other human rights groups), eliminating a generation of future revolutionaries allowed the dictatorship to set the groundwork for wealthy landowners to implement neoliberal policies and to begin selling their agricultural products to the international market. While this explanation for state terrorism is not unique to the ex-presos, only they were actually imprisoned for their beliefs and activities in liberation movements. The families of the disappeared, on the other hand, were for the most part only activated into politics after the loss of their children.

Until recently, even scholars did not focus on political prisoners. According to Ludmila da Silva Catela, the director of the Provincial Commission and Archive for Memory of Córdoba, the conspicuous absence of studies on former political prisoners in Argentina is due to human rights groups' assumption of their guilt (Da Silva Catela, June 2009). Families of the disappeared were suspicious of survivors, believing that they were remaining silent about their collaboration with the military, which allowed them to live at the expense of others (Jelin 2009, 193). Juan Carlos Álvarez, who was imprisoned for eight and a half years for his participation in a labor union and for his affiliation with the Montoneros, once said to me at an AEPPC meeting, "They disowned us twice—the military and the family members." The military disowned their actions against the ex-presos; they denied having kidnapped, tortured, and illegally detained their political opponents. And the broader human rights community also disowned the ex-presos—by denying them their victim status, by faulting them for having survived when activists' own family members did not. The marginalization of ex-presos is also demonstrated by a common phrase said during and after the dictatorship: "For some reason they were taken. For some reason they were released" (Van Drunen 2010, 170).

Many political prisoners expressed this sense of marginalization. Once at an AEPPC meeting, Gladys Regalado, who was imprisoned for four years for being a member of the PRT, explained to me: "[Families of the disappeared] discriminate against the former prisoners because they blame us for being alive." The ex-presos' marginalized status helps explain why most of those in Córdoba did not join other human rights groups after their release. Atilio Basso, who was imprisoned for four and a half years for his participation in the PRT and in labor unions, explained why he felt out of place in the group, *Familiares de Desaparecidos y Detenidos por Razones Políticas* (Families of the Disappeared and Imprisoned for Political Reasons, or *Familiares*):

> I have always been committed to solidarity movements, specifically because I am political. I never became a part of human rights organizations like Familiares because I never had a family member who was imprisoned or disappeared. There didn't seem to be a place for me. It was the same thing with the Abuelas—I don't have any grandchildren [to look for]. I wasn't actively involved in any of these groups. Instead, I was involved in various political organizations, until recently, as you know, when I was personally motivated to become a part of a group of former political prisoners. We play a role in society as the promoters of human rights, whereas Familiares is an organization specifically for family members [of the disappeared]. The fact that other human rights activists exist and are not related to the disappeared is a question that you have to ask them—the grandmothers. What about the people who are not relatives of the disappeared—what role do they have? (Basso, October 2008)

Atilio distinguishes the AEPPC from other human rights organizations by what binds each group together. He sees the ex-presos as united by their shared experience of imprisonment and of involvement in past revolutionary movements, whereas he regards the family-based human rights groups as motivated by their kinship ties to the disappeared. Yet Córdoba is the place where HIJOS, a group that includes both children of the disappeared and other activists without a blood tie, emerged. HIJOS is engaged in a range of political and social issues, in addition to their pursuit of justice for the victims. The fact that Atilio and other fellow political prisoners still distinguish themselves from other human rights groups by their commitment to politics, reveals how the various groups define and understand political commitment and activism differently. It can be easily argued that groups like the Madres are intensely political with their involvement in solving pressing social problems in Argentina. Perhaps the distinction lies in the fact that the kin-based groups have the capacity to present themselves as apolitical actors, whereas the AEPPC cannot.

Juan Carlos faced resistance from his own mother: "One day I said to her, 'I'm going to join the human rights groups.' My mom responded, 'How are you going to present yourself in front of the human rights organizations, in front of the Madres who have disappeared children?'" (Álvarez, February 2009) Juan Carlos recalled that his mother made him feel as if he was a painful reminder to the Madres that their children remained disappeared.

Because ex-presos felt excluded from human rights groups and did not have a visible status as victims, no group or individual looked after their needs for decades, despite their experiences of social discrimination and health problems. When the AEPPC became an official state organization in 2007, members themselves would often say that they were the first such group to organize, even though the *Asociación de Ex Detenidos Desaparecidos* (Association of Ex-Detainees and Disappeared, or AEDD) had formed in Buenos Aires in 1992. While both groups are made up of people who had passed through concentration camps, the AEPPC views itself as charting new territory. Ex-presos who represent Buenos Aires Province at AEPPC's national meetings do not also belong to the AEDD. According to the AEPPC members, the AEDD failed to organize or to reach out to other provinces. Some compañeros—and here I am intentionally avoiding directly attributing remarks to specific individuals—said that the AEDD was composed of collaborators, which differentiated them from the ex-presos, who were imprisoned but did not collaborate with their captors to ensure their survival. I pressed the compañeros on this distinction, but was met with few answers and could not verify these comments. In the end, these divisions are not provable and rest entirely upon gossip and speculation.

The members of the AEPPC all view themselves as having been activists prior to the dictatorship, and continue to see themselves as such. Many of the AEPPC members met each other for the first time in prison. Others knew each other only by the noms de guerre they adopted to avoid naming friends under torture. The members are, of course, not the same people they were in the 1970s and 1980s. During the 1970s, ideological differences between revolutionary groups carried more weight than they do today, since their respective organizations no longer exist. Three decades later, the former political prisoners find themselves grouping together under a commitment to claim reparations and to generally reengage in current political and social issues from a variety of political and personal viewpoints.

Yet the path to forming an organization was a long and difficult one. The marginalized status of ex-presos is not necessarily immediately apparent to outside observers. To the public, the human rights community appears as a unified front. This is particularly true in Córdoba, where the community is much smaller than the one that exists in Buenos Aires, and therefore is more likely to be in contact with each other and to hold events together. Furthermore, despite having been marginalized, the ex-presos speak positively about the other human rights groups and respect the Madres a great deal for their role in building the human rights movement. Ex-presos are quick to point out that they have benefited from the successes of the broader human rights movement. Nonetheless, there are many divisions and points of tension within the human rights community. Coming to understand the ex-presos' need to form their own organization and the ongoing marginalization of the AEPPC, was fundamental to this project, because it revealed the diversity within the victim category, particularly the fact that not all types of violations were equally weighted and therefore seen as worthy of reparation.

Buenos Aires

This project began in Buenos Aires, where I observed the commemorative events of the National Day for Memory and Justice on March 24, 2008, when I visited national memorial sites relating to the desaparecidos, including the sculptures dedicated to the disappeared at Memory Park and at the ESMA, which had once operated as a torture camp. I was interested in the roles, if any, that self-identified political prisoners occupied in these public spaces. In the traditional march through the streets of Buenos Aires to the iconic Plaza de Mayo on March 24, there was no visible group of self-identified political prisoners or survivors, while the Madres and Abuelas wore the characteristic white handkerchiefs on their heads.[4] While survivors' testimonies helped convert the ESMA into a museum, there was no explicit focus on survivors or on their experiences after their release. Similarly, no identified group of political prisoners was counted among the human rights groups behind the construction of Memory Park. The AEDD, along with the division of Madres headed by Hebe de Bonafini, refused to participate in the construction of these memorialization projects for ideological reasons; they felt that activism should be directed toward transforming Argentine political culture, rather than looking into the past (Van Drunen 2010). The absence of an organized group of survivors or political prisoners, or any presence that was explicitly publicly identifiable as such, at the annual commemorative march or at the memorialized sites, suggests how little visibility political prisoners have on the national stage.

In between my observations at these public events and spaces, I spent several hours at the Center of Legal and Social Studies' archive, collecting documents on detentions, early human rights reports on disappearances and prisons, and documentation on memorialized spaces. In addition, I followed news coverage of ongoing trials of former military officials in the two leading dailies, *Página 12* and *Clarín*, and found art exhibitions that related to the disappeared. There was no shortage of relevant organizations, books, and artworks that addressed the dictatorship era, and individual survivors had published memoirs and testimonial texts (Timerman 1998[1981]; Partnoy 1986; Calviero 1998). However, the collective public voice of political prisoners was lacking.

During one of my visits to the office of Familiares to copy archival documents, I had one short interaction that revealed more about the position that political prisoners inhabited in the human rights movement than all of my other research excursions in Buenos Aires combined. After receiving an invitation over the phone to visit the Familiares office, I went to meet Hugo Argente, a staff member and former political prisoner who had been imprisoned for searching for his disappeared brother, Julio Daniel. On my second visit to the office, Hugo told me to take a seat at the large conference table while he made a phone call.

"What was the name of the compañera in Córdoba that you are working with?"

"Sara Waitman."

Hugo picked up the phone and began dialing. At this point, I wasn't sure if I was privy to the conversation, and I tried to occupy myself with my fieldnotes. However, since Hugo was not standing far from the table, I couldn't help but listen in on a few parts of the conversation, particularly when he said my name and Sara's. He hung up.

"Everything okay?" I said.

"Yes, I called the Familiares office in Córdoba, and they know Sara. They know her well. She's a good compañera. But their relationship with the ex-presos isn't very good."

"Oh?" I paused. "Should I be worried? What is wrong?"

"There's always *quilombos* (shitstorms)." And Hugo waved his hand before retrieving an archival file that turned out to belong to his own disappeared brother.

At the beginning of my research, human rights activists would talk about solidarity among the human rights groups and the ways in which they often supported each other's efforts. Even so, I had been warned by researchers from the U.S. National Security Archive in Washington, D.C., that building ties with any particular group might make it hard to ingratiate myself with others. I knew that it would be difficult to dig out honest answers, especially about conflicts between human rights organizations, not to mention the AEPPC or similar organizations of political prisoners. I asked several AEPPC members about Hugo's comment and whether it was true, and I was told that the conflict between them and the other human rights organizations was complicated, but that there were partnerships and positive individual relationships between members of Familiares and HIJOS. Many of the political prisoners' own children were part of HIJOS. Still, others mentioned in vague terms that a clash in personalities among a few individuals made the relationship "complicated." This complicated relationship led to other questions about why the political prisoners in Córdoba felt compelled to start their own group, and what the political prisoners did before the AEPPC formed in 2008. The origins of the AEPPC are related to questions about who were defined as the primary victims of the dictatorship, and what violations were considered to be worthy of reparation—both symbolic and financial.

Córdoba

As soon as I arrived in Córdoba, I realized that the city's status as the second largest in Argentina was misleading. The difference between the cities of Córdoba and Buenos Aires is quite significant, mostly because Córdoba feels provincial. People in Córdoba would often say that they were from the "interior" and were "more warm and affectionate" than the "arrogant Porteños"—those who were born in Buenos Aires, the port city. Just as Porteños are known for their unique accents, Córdobeses are known for their lyrical drawl. In Córdoba, the human rights community is far smaller and, perhaps for that reason, more collaborative; many of the main actors overlapped at the time of research. There was no active branch of Madres and only one active Abuela, Sonia Torres, whose elegance and educated background inspired admiration. The two most active human rights groups were HIJOS and Familiares, and they shared an office. Both HIJOS and Familiares were founded in Córdoba.

My connection to the AEPPC rested upon Waitman, the group's president. She had been imprisoned with Irene Martínez, a political exile and medical doctor in Chicago who had originally put me on the path to study political prisoners. Irene and I had met at a human rights conference in 2007, where she told me that her compañeros were facing serious health and economic problems and that more attention needed to be drawn to their plight. Irene had contacted Sara about the possibility that I would be able to work with the AEPPC, and the group had taken a vote about my presence, which was approved.

When I first arrived in Córdoba, Sara and I had arranged to meet after I visited the *Comision y el Archivo Provincial de la Memoria de Cordoba* (Provincial Commission and Archive of Memory of Córdoba, also known as the *Archivo*), and the site where the former *Departmento de Informaciónes de la Policía de la Provincia de Córdoba* (Center for Police Intelligence for the Province of Córdoba, or D2) had operated as a clandestine detention center in the 1970s and 1980s. The Archivo is located in the main town square, Plaza San Martín, and resides within the historic *cabildo* (town hall) building. It sits right next to the main Jesuit cathedral, and the space between these two buildings—which was closed to the public until the Archivo opened in 2006—is referred to as *Pasaje Santa Catalina* (Santa Catalina Passage). Now

that this passage is open, hundreds walk from other main street thoroughfares and from nearby shopping districts to the front of the Archivo.

Though I had already met most of the AEPPC members in Buenos Aires at
other events, I felt that my first visit to the Archivo was the official beginning
of my meetings with AEPPC members. I was told to ask for Stella "Estelita"
Molina, a compañera who was "very skinny." While Estelita never opened up
to me about her experiences over the duration of my fieldwork and refused
to be interviewed, she did offer me books, invite me to her home, and tell
me how to properly make *empanadas* (meat pies)—after declaring my first
batch too dry and lacking in onions. Estelita gave me my first tour of the
Archivo, quizzed me on my research intentions, and then sent me off to
meet Sara and Gladys Regalado, the latter who was another compañera and
Sara's best friend, for *carlitos* (panini sandwiches) and coffee.

It was then that Sara explained that the AEPPC was in the process of
working on four main projects. The first was the first-ever health census
of political prisoners in Córdoba Province, which would be useful in assessing the needs of fellow political prisoners. Another area that the AEPPC was
working toward was supporting trials against former military officials, both
by contributing their own testimonies and by simply attending the trials to
underscore the importance of legal justice. They repeatedly made several
public announcements in demand of the reappearance of former political
prisoner Jorge Julio López, who disappeared on September 18, 2006, after
giving his testimony as a witness in the case against Miguel Etchecolatz, a
former senior police officer guilty of committing genocidal acts during the
dictatorship. A third area was loosely termed *educación* (education), which
involved speaking at public venues about what had happened to political
prisoners and to their disappeared compañeros, a book of testimonies that
they were in the process of putting together, and work at the Archivo. The
AEPPC was particularly interested in transmitting their memories to the
young generation. Lastly, the AEPPC focused on solidarity with their compañeros and their families by way of gaining *efectiva reparación histórica*
(effective historical reparation). This involved lobbying various politicians
to pass a law that would provide financial reparations to political prisoners, in addition to what had been distributed in the 1990s. The recipients
had deemed the first set of reparations insufficient, both financially and
symbolically.

At the time of my fieldwork, the political prisoners did not have their own meeting place. Most of my fieldwork took place in the Archivo because it was often a gathering place for the political prisoners and for other human rights activists in Córdoba. The Archivo was also one of three sites where the AEPPC administered its provincial census of political prisoners; the other two were located on the fourth floor of the Secretariat of Human Rights and on the top floor of the Familiares office. Every Saturday, I attended AEPPC's weekly meeting in the borrowed space of the Light and Power Union's building. Other places where I spent time with the various individual political prisoners were at cafés and in their homes, as well as at rallies, lobby visits, trial sessions, and public events relating to either labor unions or local political issues.

I had chosen an extraordinarily lucky time to be in Córdoba. I was there when the political prisoners felt that they had finally established themselves within the human rights community and when several new human rights developments took place. Sara had explained when I first met the ex-presos in May 2008, that then secretary of human rights, Luis Duhalde, had agreed to receive a representative group of political prisoners for the first time. They had been requesting meetings since 2003, but had never been extended an invitation. My arrival in Córdoba also coincided with the first trial against former military officials to take place there. I was present when several of the AEPPC's projects got off the ground, including the census; the final draft of their edited volume of testimonies; and the opening of a former torture camp, La Perla, to visitors. I was also there at a time when the members of the AEPPC were united on various issues and there was general consensus within the organization. Since I left, three members passed away from illnesses, several others underwent major surgeries, and serious conflicts arose between the members. Still, the positions that I present genuinely reflect a general consensus among the members, unless stated otherwise.

It cannot be stated enough that Sara Waitman is an extraordinary leader, and that I benefited from her introductions into the human rights community in Córdoba. She served two terms as president of the AEPPC and was unique in her ability both to build consensus within the group, and to build bridges with other human rights activists and family-based human rights groups. Quick to solve conflicts, Sara would find innovative ways to bring people together, as well as to find points of shared interest between various groups within the human rights community. Not all of the compañeros enjoyed her easy relationships with other human rights groups, but both men and women within the AEPPC respected her. When I first introduced myself to the AEPPC, I explained the purpose and subject of my research. As soon as I finished, Sara explained to her compañeros that I wasn't simply going to study them, but that I had been recommended by a fellow compañera, Irene Martínez, and that I was going to assist them on all of their projects. After Sara spoke, the political prisoners nodded their heads and showed their approval. My connections and solidarity were more important than my research questions. Although the AEPPC had already voted on my project before I even traveled to Argentina, I still had to prove that I had compatible views and that I was not, in fact, part of the CIA. "Why would a young American woman want to hang out with us old folks?" said AEPPC member Sebastián Cannizzo, at the end of one of the first weekly meetings.

Sara had me visit the Archivo as my introduction into the community, and it was surprising to learn shortly thereafter that the political prisoners were not technically official members of the Archivo. The official members included the Abuelas, Familiares, HIJOS, *Servicio Paz y Justicia* (Service of Peace and Justice), *Universidad Nacional Córdoba* (National University of Córdoba), provincial executive branch representatives, provincial legislative branch representatives, and provincial justice branch representatives, several of which had a much less significant presence in the local human rights scene. Not being an official member when the Archivo was first established meant that the AEPPC did not benefit from the government subsidy that all of the other members received, and that they were not officially listed as members in the legal document that established the Archivo on March 22, 2006 (Law No. 9286). By the end of my fieldwork, however, the AEPPC's status had changed and it joined the list of organizations. However, the initial exclusion was reflective of the political prisoners' position as not-quite-established members of the human rights community.

The fact that all thirty-nine political prisoners interviewed felt that they had been ignored by both society and by the human rights community drew my attention toward the question of why they were not seen as primary victims of the dictatorship, while the relatives of the disappeared were. Two months after I arrived in Córdoba, I learned through casual conversations that no one had yet recorded the testimonies of AEPPC members. I proposed creating the group's first oral history archive to AEPPC member Alicia Staps, who quickly agreed and suggested that I propose it at the next weekly meeting. Once the AEPPC agreed to the idea by vote, I collected interview questions from the AEPPC members during three consecutive weekly meetings. I circulated a piece of paper and members anonymously wrote questions for me to include in the interviews. These questions generated the majority of the content of the oral history interviews. In addition to this list of questions, I added two more: what they felt was the most important effort that the government undertook for survivors, and why they felt that they needed their own organization. The final chapter explains why the types of violations that the political prisoners consider the most significant, were not addressed by the transitional justice efforts in Argentina. I also discovered that members felt that the marginalization that they had suffered over the past few decades culminated in health and economic challenges as they aged, spurring them to form an organization to address their needs and those of their compañeros, rather than to join Familiares or another established human rights group.

The AEPPC Petitions for Legal Status

A few months after the oral history project began, I interviewed Alicia in her home. I was particularly proud of my relationship with Alicia, since she was underwhelmed by my presence when I first met her in Buenos Aires at the AEPPC lobby visits. "Who is she?" she had asked when I showed up at their meeting. Sara told her who I was, and Alicia immediately walked away. However, several months later, we had established a good relationship; she was a passionate and highly educated person who enjoyed teaching me about Argentine history and sharing her opinions about neoliberalism and about her disdain for the United States.

Toward the end of our interview, when I asked Alicia why the political prisoners petitioned for *personería jurídica* (legal status) from the government, she spoke beyond the practicalities. With legal status, the AEPPC could request and receive state funding for conferences and travel, submit resolutions to the local government, and participate in public rallies and forums as a state-recognized group. Unlike the others, Alicia also said that the AEPPC petitioned for personería jurídica to become a member of the Archivo. Without it, they had been told that they could not be part of the official list of organizations as stated in the law. Alicia remembered the moment when she learned that the AEPPC had been excluded.

Before the AEPPC existed, Alicia had been part of Familiares. The only other political prisoner she remembered being involved in the group at that point was Sara, who, Alicia said, "did not have any family members [who were disappeared] but had a boyfriend who was disappeared—Nona D'Ambra" (Staps, November 2008). Sara and Alicia quickly became friends, and Alicia soon immersed herself in Familiares and in its activities, just as Sara did. Alicia recalled a meeting that took place in 2006, while she was at the Familiares office, where Dr. Martín Fresnada[5] announced that legislation was underway for the creation of the Archivo. Dr. Fresnada was one of the lawyers representing Familiares in bringing former military officials to trial in Córdoba as well as the son of two disappeared parents, and he knew that the new law would be approved. "After he recited the law's contents, they all stood up applauding, while I sat still like this," said Alicia, sitting across from me with her back straight, her body tense, and her hands gripping the edges of her chair (Ibid.). She continued:

> Sara stood up, applauded—the whole world did. Sara said, "Yes!" But she hadn't realized what was going on, because if she had, she would have reacted in the same way that I did. I remained still like this, and then the yeast started to rise [i.e., I became angry]. I waited for Martin to go upstairs and then I went after him. I followed him up the stairs and said to him, "Explain to me something: Why aren't the former political prisoners in the Commission [and Archive] of Memory?"
>
> "Because you don't have it."
>
> "What are you talking about?"
>
> "Personería jurídica."
>
> "What did you say?" I said to him, "If all of you [HIJOS] don't have personería jurídica, then you aren't included either. HIJOS can't use the same one as Familiares."

"Yes, but it's different. We are under Familiares'—you all have nothing; you are a commission that meets but you don't have any kind of organization." (Ibid.)

Up until the Archivo was created, there was no particular need for ex-presos to petition for legal status. The ex-presos were political activists, not an institution, or at least not one affiliated with the state; they had relied upon their previous organizing methods to support labor unions, trials, and their own memory projects. The ex-presos spoke at local schools and shared their personal experiences as individual volunteers, not through any formal organization. The state had never required survivors to be a part of any legal group to contribute testimonies to the 1984 truth commission report, nor before paying out economic reparations to survivors in the 1990s. Alicia continued her story:

Then at that point, I got real angry and it set me off, because I said to him, "Your father and your mother did not need a law or legal status to give birth to you and dedicate themselves to fighting the system, and I don't either. I don't need legal status to be an activist!" I was terrible, really terrible, but it incensed me. It made me lose my temper. . . ." A big blowup ensued—I was crying; Martín was crying; the two of us were crying. And then Sara came and the HIJOS kids started in on the fight. I insulted everyone—I was furious. I told them, "Who do you think you are? We are the survivors. We have the memories that you depend on—we are the memory, and we are not in the Commission of Memory. How can you do this to us, you filthy brats! You didn't consider us, even though you know it's us." Look, I told them all of this when I was really angry; I was so furious. I went downstairs and when I went below, everybody was there, they and the whole world were *chocho*.[6] I called, "Sara." I grabbed Sara. "Come here—did you see what just happened?"

And she said to me, "What? Why are you like this?"

And I told her, "Did you not see that they didn't include us, the former political prisoners?"

"Of course," she said to me, "Yes, of course I realized."

A lie—because clearly she hadn't realized, or she would have responded the same way. Only in that moment, did she come to her senses and said, "All right, but stay calm—we're going to see what we can do about it." No, it wasn't something to remain calm about! (Ibid.)

After this incident, Alicia said a group of compañeros initiated the process of gaining legal status, which they were subsequently granted in 2007. (The resolution that created the Archivo passed into law in 2006.) I pressed Alicia further on why, aside from being part of the Archivo, the AEPPC needed its own particular official organization, rather than working through Familiares, like HIJOS:

Why? Because they had to get together in order to collect their indemnifications and they [the government] had never done any-thing for the compañeros. That is something that the rest of the human rights organizations—this is an excellent question—threw in our face and told us, "When we the mothers were doing activism and making rounds around the Plaza de Mayo, and the kids in HIJOS organized, the Abuelas organized to reclaim their grandchildren, you were doing nothing." It's very simple, because they weren't prisoners, neither tortured, nor persecuted, nor disappeared; they were the family members, not [the disappeared]; they weren't look-ing for them; they had jobs; they had lives; they had a family; they had one desaparecido, or two, let's say, but had a full life. With us, they destroyed our families. They took away our identities. We couldn't get jobs. We led persecuted lives. We were forced to live clandestinely, hiding ourselves; the majority of us were discrimi-nated against for having been guerrillas or political prisoners, for what happened to us, for being kidnapped, or whatever it was they came for; they persecuted us from all sides. They came after us with sticks; with sticks they beat us up from all sides—how were we going to organize under these conditions, if the only thing we could do was save our lives? (Ibid.)

Though members of Madres, Abuelas, and Familiares were at risk of dis-appearance when they first began organizing, and some were even killed or tortured, the former political prisoners felt discriminated against even after the dictatorship fell from power. Prior to the formation of the AEPPC, the members had already been in labor unions, community organizations, and political groups. But the AEPPC members felt that no one was actively addressing their needs as survivors in post-dictatorship Argentina.

Victim Status in Four Phases

At the Congreso Provincial de Ex-Presos Políticos de Córdoba (Provincial Conference for Former Political Prisoners) held in Córdoba capital in February 2009, AEPPC member Élida "Ely" Eichenberger described four different phases in which political prisoners' victim statuses fluctuated—a summary that her fellow compañeros agreed with at the meeting. Ely repeated this claim in her oral history archive interview, when she outlined the first phase as follows: "Well, since the seventies until the eighties, '83, let's say, we were—or '85—the ugly, the bad, and the dirty. That is, we were the fucking guerrillas; we were the ones who put the country in crisis, etc. etc." (Eichenberger, October 2008). The first phase began when activists were hunted down by the military and ended with the initial efforts of President Alfonsín's government to address the crimes committed under the dictatorship. Ely's timeline reflects the twin facts that political violence preceded the 1976 takeover and that the early transitional justice efforts did not redeem ex-presos in the public eye. By dating the first phase from the beginning of the 1970s, Ely acknowledges that political prisoners had a history of activism prior to the coup in '76, and that the dictatorship targeted activists in addition to random innocent youths. But their activism was seen to justify, or to explain, why they were taken by the military.

Ely describes the second period as a radical shift from being depicted as terrorists, to being seen as helpless victims: "Afterward came another phase that was the phase of the organizations, where we were the poor, pathetic ones who the military tortured" (Ibid.). Ely is referring to the period in which the family-based human rights groups dominated the transitional justice process and spoke about the desaparecidos in terms of the torture they endured rather than their political activities.

Ely continued with the third period. "After this came the idea, the Two Demons Theory. That is, the military was bad because we had been bad. That is, we returned to being the ugly, the bad and the dirty" (Ibid.). Ely argues that even as political prisoners were seen as victims in the truth commission and in the early trials, the official narrative distinguished them from the disappeared, who were the "real" (innocent, apolitical) victims. Instead, the former political prisoners were seen as responsible for bringing state violence upon themselves.

Since then, Ely argued, during the past two decades, the resurgence of memory projects and renewed trials have changed the overall political climate in favor of the survivors. Increasingly, survivors began publishing their own accounts in the late 1990s and 2000s. With the public support of former president Néstor Kirchner and his wife, President Cristina Fernández de Kirchner, the ex-presos became less demonized and increasingly acknowledged as victims of state terrorism. Yet families of the disappeared still stigmatized survivors over the circumstances of their reappearance.

Ely concluded by telling her fellow compañeros that they now had the space to define themselves, which could be considered the fourth phase: "I think, this is the time, in that —we, the former political prisoners, have to position ourselves in a different place in history. That is, we are not innocent. We had a project for the country. . . . We had a lot of strength, and really we had an economic and social and political proposal"(Ibid.).

This history of the marginalization of survivors can easily be forgotten when observing the human rights movement in Argentina today. The presence of a national network of former political prisoners can be read as just another step in the longer history of activism among victims, but a more honest inspection reveals tensions and suspicions, which arose in part due to how the human rights framework was mobilized and defined early on. The changing status of ex-presos could be summed up in the following way: they were first seen as terrorists, second as victims, third as deserving what had happened to them, and finally, as "victims of state terrorism" who also seek to maintain their activist identities. The achievements that the families of the disappeared have made in their pursuit for "memory, truth, and justice" over the past three decades, have indeed created an aperture for new actors in the field of human rights, including ones who had once been marginalized. Thus, the formation of the AEPPC is, in fact, new to the longer history of human rights and to the transitional justice process in Argentina. For the ex-presos, their coming together was as much as a response to what happened to them during the dictatorship, as to what happened to them afterward

3

Suspicion and Collaboration

Not all victims are the same. Take, for example, South Africa's Truth and Reconciliation Commission, which had difficulties in drawing lines between victims and perpetrators during apartheid, particularly since there were varying levels of innocence and guilt within each category (Borer 2003). Heroes became perpetrators, and perpetrators became victims. Some African National Congress members who were victims of gross human rights violations, including torture, were also accused of committing acts of violence in their fight for liberation. The activist, Winnie Mandela, who was also the second wife of South Africa's first black president, Nelson Mandela, was banned and tortured under apartheid but was then later accused of committing human rights abuses herself.

In Argentina, the military and its supporters made similar accusations against the former political prisoners, claiming that they were perpetrators of violence and not simply fighting for liberation from capitalism. In fact, families of the military and police forces claim that their relatives are also political prisoners who are now being victimized by the left-wing activists who have assumed power in the post-dictatorship era. However, not all victims under Argentina's dictatorship were politically involved or armed guerrillas, which raises the question: should a left-wing guerrilla be considered less of a victim than those torture victims who had no political involvement? Political prisoners are not only regarded as terrorists by some sectors of Argentine society, but they are also perceived differently than the disappeared even by human rights activists. Members of the family-based human rights groups have perpetuated the myth that those who died had given themselves over to the greater struggle, while survivors broke under torture. This chapter explores the question of whether or not ex-presos have a lesser victim status than do the disappeared.

AEPPC members believe that they have been blamed for the deaths of the disappeared by the victims' families. The charge made against survivors is that they made compromises while held prisoner that came at the expense of their compañeros. Whether or not the accusations are true, the suggestion that political prisoners may have collaborated with the military impacted survivors' integration into the human rights movement. In turn, survivors' exclusion from the human rights movement later accounted for their lower visibility at sites of former torture camps that now function as memorial museums, or at institutions that commemorate historical incidents of mass violence and that have an "uneasy conceptual coexistence of reverent remembrance and critical interpretation" (Williams 2007, 8). The families of the disappeared have long been considered the primary victims and, as a result, they are seen to have a claim of ownership over these memorial museums (Jelin 2009). Yet, AEPPC members desire concrete roles as tour guides at memorial museums, in part as a reaction to their feelings of exclusion from these types of memory-making projects. This desire highlights the differential social treatment of different groups of victims in Argentina. As we will see, ex-presos are seen as traitors, and the disappeared as heroes. Based on the experiences of post-apartheid South Africa, Government and International Relations scholar, Tristan Anne Borer, in "A Taxonomy of Victims and Perpetrators: Human Rights and Reconciliation in South Africa" (2003) warns against the desire to think in absolutes and instead advocates a grayer landscape in order to think about the complexity of violence and the actors within the conflict.

In addition to discussing the dichotomy between desaparecidos and survivors in Argentina, I will also introduce another gray area: the AEPPC's distinction within the survivor category between collaborators (with the military) and noncollaborators in torture camps. This division is relevant to broader debates of who should direct memorialized spaces and how to present sites of terror (Williams 2007). If the goal is to strive to maintain a gray landscape in order to capture the complexity of the past, then it is important to make more explicit, the internal divisions that the political prisoners and families of the disappeared draw within the victim category. I argue that the presence of political prisoners at the memorial museums increases the possibility of speaking about the gray areas of victim categories because it allows survivors to speak about the reasons behind their imprisonment. The dual presence of the disappeared in the imaginations of visitors at memorialized sites, and of the survivors as guides in the same sites, creates a pathway to think and to speak about complicated categories of victim and perpetrator.

There are several distinctions made by human rights activists, the media, and international human rights groups within the victim category in Argentina. For instance, while there is no official hierarchy of victims, it is no coincidence that people both in Argentina and abroad know the name of Dagmar Hagelin, the seventeen-year-old Swedish Argentine citizen who was disappeared after being mistaken for someone else. Meanwhile, no particular name of any former member of armed revolutionary groups would be as recognizable. The AEPPC members, who were all rank-and-file members of labor unions and revolutionary groups, were not only considered guerrillas—and therefore less than innocent in comparison to victims without any political background—but they also rank lower than the disappeared and their relatives by virtue of their survival. Survivors with political backgrounds occupy the bottom rung of this unofficial categorization of victims because they are seen as *traidores* (traitors) who gave away their compañeros in exchange for their survival. That is, both the collective and the dream of liberation were more important than the individual, and survival itself is seen as evidence of engagement in various acts of collaboration with the military, which implies that survivors gave up on the collective and the dream altogether.

Ana Longoni's (2007) *Traiciones: La figura del traidor en los relatos acerca de los sobrevivientes de la represión* (Treacheries: The figure of the traitor in stories about the survivors of the repression), one of the few books on the subject of survivors, is even more unique since it addresses the accusation that survivors betrayed the revolutionary cause. In analyzing three fictional accounts in which the figure of survivor as traitor appears—Miguel Bonasso's (1984) *Recuerdo de la muerte* (Memory of death), Rolo Diez's (2000) *Los compañeros* (The compañeros), and Liliana Heker's (1996) *El fin de la historia* (The end of the story)—Longoni proposes five theories as to why survivors of Argentina's dictatorship are assumed to have won their reappearance through some kind of betrayal, and therefore are considered to be traitors. The first theory she suggests is that the survivors remind families that the majority of the victims were systematically murdered. Second, the disappeared were first seen as innocent and apolitical, and then later as national heroes. The survivors, however, muddle the idealized figure of the desaparecido when they speak about their complicated experiences within revolutionary movements. As a result, the survivors are marked as traitors rather than as heroes, which, in effect, erases their status as victims. Third, the survival strategies of some of the survivors might have distanced them from the hero/martyr figure attached to the desaparecidos. Fourth, there is a general absence of critical debate about the political movements of the 1970s, and by extension, there is no critical context in which to understand the disappeared and the survivors. The fifth and final hypothesis that Longoni proposes, is that the failure of the revolutionary dream falls upon the survivors. The disappeared are assumed to have given themselves up to the struggle to their fullest capacity, while the survivors are seen as failing to do so.

Longoni disputes the dichotomy between the hero and traitor as overly simplistic and reductionist, and she utilizes Primo Levi's concept of the gray zone, in *The Drowned and the Saved* (1989[1986]) to understand the actual experiences of imprisonment and torture. Furthermore, she wonders to what extent these authors can understand the survivors' experiences without having undergone it themselves, and she observes that all three naturalize the dichotomy between hero and traitor. Ultimately, Longoni calls for a more open and humanistic view toward the survivor experience, including the contradictions and complications of having belonged to revolutionary movements and having survived within a context of severe dehumanization.

Longoni's articulation of the dichotomy between the disappeared and survivors helps explain the differences within the category of victim in Argentina. By virtue of being dead, the disappeared are seen as the most victimized, and the family members who lost them, are the most victimized in the post-dictatorial period. Among the victims taken to the camps and prisons, the young and apolitical are more tragically mourned as undeserving, even though their later political activism is read as an act of martyrdom. Longoni's analysis builds on the idea of the gray zone, yet my personal conversations with the AEPPC members and my observations of discussions that took place in weekly meetings, illustrate that these particular political prisoners drew a stark distinction between themselves and those who collaborated. Thus, while the ex-presos criticize the dichotomy between the desaparecidos and survivors for presenting the former as good and the latter as "damned"—as AEPPC member Élida "Ely" Eichenberger would say—they ironically reinforce another dichotomy of good and bad as they attempt to distance themselves from the image of the collaborating survivor. Many ex-presos regard themselves differently than their compañeros who have been accused of collaboration, but, at the same time, they contradictorily suggest that no one outside of the camps has a right to judge the actions taken under such extreme conditions. Ex-presos view themselves as the opposite of traitors: steadfast activists who remained politically involved despite the military's attempts to silence them through fear and torture. But by distinguishing themselves from collaborating survivors and by disputing the accusations made against them, the ex-presos inadvertently marginalize fellow compañeros in their quest to redeem themselves as committed activists in prison and in their participation in the human rights movement today.

Collaborators versus Noncollaborators

While attending the trial against former third army corps Gen. Luciano Benjamín Menéndez and seven of his sub-officials in Córdoba in May 2008, I regularly listened to the ex-presos reflect upon the performances of the lawyers, witnesses, and judges after each day's proceedings were called to a close. The trial centered on four victims who were disappeared, tortured, and ultimately killed at La Perla, the largest concentration camp that operated in Córdoba Province. On one occasion, while walking home from the Federal Tribunal Building to the city center, I spoke with "Daniel,"[1] a former political prisoner who said that the types of witnesses who testified meant that the audience members were not hearing the complete story. Daniel said that the witnesses who testified were collaborators, which reinforced the perception that all of the survivors were collaborators. In other conversations with several AEPPC members, I asked why they were not serving as witnesses in this trial, and they explained to me that they had been hooded their whole duration in La Perla, so they could not visually identify the men on trial. Only collaborators, they explained, could serve as useful witnesses. In order to perform the duties of collaboration, which ranged from cleaning up blood and other bodily fluids after interrogation sessions, to identifying other potential victims by riding in cars with military officers, the captives were able to see.

This distinction between collaborators and noncollaborators was important to this AEPPC member, because he felt that academics often overlooked this difference. Recalling an argument that Daniel had with scholars on the topic of collaboration with the military, he recounted how one prominent scholar argued in favor of withholding judgment because of the moral ambiguities of the situation. Daniel disagreed because he knew of captives who had refused to collaborate and still survived, himself included. He went on to clarify that noncollaborator survivors were not necessarily of better moral character, or more committed to the revolutionary cause. In other words, it was not a matter of saying that some compañeros were better or worse than others, but that the ethical choice that these ex-presos made should be distinguished and honored differently than those who did collaborate with the military, and that not all survivors should be assumed to have collaborated.

Part of the reason why Daniel was careful about making value judgments was because he said that not every prisoner was held under the same circumstances. Using himself as an example, he said that because he was only nineteen years old and did not have any children or a spouse, it was easier for him to refuse collaboration; he had less to lose, though his parents could have been threatened. Other prisoners were made to choose between having a family member tortured, and collaborating with the military in some form or another. He also pointed out that some were never asked to collaborate, and therefore never had to make that kind of decision. Yet, he maintained, it should not be lost that those who were asked to collaborate faced an ethical dilemma that was literally a matter of life and death, and that their survival should not diminish the risk they took in refusing.

In recorded conversations among five women-survivors of the ESMA in Buenos Aires that were published in *That Inferno* (2006), by Munu Actis,

Cristina Aldini, Liliana Gardella, Minam Lewin, and Elisa Tokar, three of the survivors explained that victims' resistance under torture depended on when someone "fell" into the hands of the military. Before the official start of the dictatorship, captives were unaware of the chances of being disappeared and were more capable of withstanding torture without "singing," or giving up information:

MUNÚ [ACTIS]: It seems to me that, from the standpoint of the deterioration, it was one thing to *fall* in 1976, another thing in 1978, and quite another in 1980. Your level of deterioration in 1976, was much less than in 1978.

MIRIAM [LEWIN]: Not to mention 1974 and 1975! The people who *fell* then almost never *sang*.

ELISA [TOKAR]: They never *sang*, and they really fucked them up! But you had something inside you.

MIRIAM [LEWIN]: That fire, that certainty of victory, the feeling that Utopia was within your grasp. (Actis et al. 2006, 280, italics in the original)

Seventeen of the AEPPC members interviewed fell before the dictatorship, while fourteen fell in 1976, five in 1977, and another three in 1978. Though the AEPPC members did not speak about the date of their fall as an important factor in withholding information in their interviews, the theory proposed by the ESMA survivors may account for why these ex-presos claim not to have collaborated with the military. Slightly less than half fell before the dictatorship, but most fell early enough, so that it's very likely they had not been aware of the risks. The three women who fell in 1978, were considered to be *muy comprometida* (very committed) to the cause. Two of them lost family members during the dictatorship, one disappeared and the other executed.

The place in which victims were held also may account for the ex-presos' ability to refuse to collaborate. In the final chapter of *That Inferno*, the five ESMA survivors invited a former political prisoner, Mirta Clara, to analyze the differences between the concentration camps and prisons. Mirta observes that captives in prisons were able to organize themselves despite the military's attempt to destroy their group identity, whereas in concentration camps, the kidnappers' goal involved "taking over and destroying the bodies" (Ibid., 290). Without being able to band together, it was harder to resist collaboration in the concentration camps. In camps, victims endured extreme physical torture, such as electric shock. In prisons, while there were violent confrontations and various psychological forms of torture, not to mention living in solitary cells with poor diets, the level of violence varied. Another major difference was that camps meant a higher likelihood of death; AEPPC members recalled being relieved when they were transferred from a camp to a prison. Life in camps was far more precarious: prisoners did not know if they were going to live the next day, and they were unsure if a fellow prisoner was a collaborator who could turn them in, or a compañero who would help them survive. The different levels of compromise or strategies employed to survive did not necessarily lead to a definitive separation between those who were held in camps and those in regular prisons, but it explains why some believe refusal was not an option for those held in camps. Almost all of the AEPPC members passed through camps before being transferred to a regular prison; only three ex-presos did not pass through a camp.

The collaborator question not only impacted how all of the survivors were treated in the post-dictatorship era, but it has also posed a challenge for the human rights community regarding who should play a role in memorialized spaces. That is, it is not a simply a matter of agreeing to have survivors work at memorial museums; it also means deciding which survivors should have an official staff role. As argued previously, the marginalization of ex-presos is due precisely to the suspicion that all who survived, collaborated. While one solution in overcoming this marginalization is to accept all survivors—to emphasize the fact that one cannot judge another for trying to survive in the most extreme and inhumane conditions—many AEPPC members want to maintain the distinction between collaborators and other survivors by choosing who will guide tours at memorial museums.

In the memorialized spaces of D2 (now the Archivo) and La Perla, in Córdoba, where staff positions have been allotted to ex-presos, the AEPPC must decide who among its membership should fill one of these highly coveted jobs. This decision-making process is extremely sensitive and challenging, in part because all of the AEPPC's decisions are based on consensus and require every member to weigh in on the matter. At weekly meetings, members add their names to a speaking list and take turns sharing information or opinions until there is no one else left to speak. Meetings often last for several hours. When nominating an ex-preso for a paid position, such as working on the census, the AEPPC members mutually agreed that the candidate must possess at least two qualifications: *política* and financial need. Política roughly translates to "politics" and means having political consciousness, knowledge of social movements, and firsthand experience as an active participant in a social movement, as well as supporting the common political goals of the group. The política requirement ensures that the tour guide's disposition will fall in line with the rest of the ex-preso community. As for the latter qualification, financial need is determined by looking at a variety of markers, including income, home ownership, number of (dependent or supportive) children, general health, past history of unemployment, and economic status in comparison to the rest of the ex-presos.

When one of the witnesses who testified against former general Menéndez expressed interest in working as a guide at La Perla, a heated debate ensued among the AEPPC members. The other human rights groups in Córdoba ultimately supported her nomination—after all, she had played a key role as a witness in the first trial of former military officials in Córdoba. Most of the members of the AEPPC, however, felt differently about her working at La Perla. During the AEPPC meeting, when the bulk of this debate took place, several members said that while they appreciated this survivor's testimony in the trial, allowing her to work as a tour guide violated the memory of those who died there, and was an insult to those who survived but who did not collaborate. The military committed such terrible crimes, some AEPPC members felt, that to have a collaborator work as a human rights representative, would minimize the actions of those who had refused to save their own lives through collaboration.

As one AEPPC member present at the meeting said of the witness, "I welcome her into the trial and recognize her efforts, but I will not share a mate with her." In Argentine culture, sipping the herbal tea mate is a sign of friendship because a group of friends will drink out of the same gourd. This former political prisoner recognized the utility of collaborators in trials but did not see them as compañeros, or even as worthy of inclusion in a basic social ritual. Though some compañeros at the meeting were willing to consider the witness as a fellow worker because she too was a survivor, the final vote went against her appointment.

The task of choosing who should speak at memorialized spaces is a contested one for the AEPPC members precisely because not all victims are regarded the same by human rights groups, and not all survivors see themselves as equal with all others in terms of collaboration. It is not simply about dismantling the dichotomies between victim and perpetrator, between disappeared and survivor, but it is also about the survivors who see differences among them, between those who collaborated and those who did not, between those who passed through camps and those who spent time in regular prisons. By distinguishing themselves from collaborating survivors, the noncollaborating ones, the ex-presos in the AEPPC, can deny the accusations made by the families of the disappeared that they had betrayed their compañeros. Yet, families of the disappeared may overlook this distinction when considering that collaborating survivors provide legal testimonies crucial to bringing former military officials responsible for the deaths of their loved ones to trial.

Narration and Memorial Museums

Memorial museums depart from conventional norms that museums usually embody: they pay respect to the dead, contradict narratives of the previous regime, seek to make sense of violence, and provide an experience for visitors to feel something about the events that took place (Williams 2007). For the purposes of presenting former CCDs that now function as memorial museums, Argentine survivors—whether they collaborated or not—are instrumental to understanding how the spaces were used and in knowing what happened to whom, by whom, and when. In fact, collaborators with the military may tell us more about these spaces because of their role in the apparatus at the time of their imprisonment. While the AEPPC took an official stance against employing a known collaborator at La Perla, the real challenge of narrating memorial museums in Argentina may have to do with whether survivors are giving the tours at all. In comparing two memorial museums, one in Buenos Aires and the other in Córdoba, I found that the absence of survivors meant that the tours focused on human rights abuses in the camps and reinforced the image of the disappeared as heroic martyrs, or as innocent victims. Conversely, when survivors were directing the tours, emphasis was placed on the reasons for disappearances and imprisonment. Furthermore, within the context of survivors having been read as traitors and therefore stigmatized, survivors speaking about themselves as committed activists then and now, represented a significant step toward elevating the status of the reappeared.

In what follows, I take us through two memorial museums, with the purpose of showing that the presence of a survivor, such as an AEPPC member, presents a wider view of victims by juxtaposing two of the categories of victims in one place. The disappeared are remembered in these spaces as victims of torture through testimonial accounts and through the memories of others, and the political prisoners speak about the reasons behind their disappearance and offer visitors a chance to ask about their participation in social movements and their survival.

The ESMA in Buenos Aires: A Memorial Without Survivors

The Argentine state established the ESMA as a memorial museum in 2004, and renamed it the *Espacio para la Memoria y para la Promoción y Defensa de los Derechos Humanos* (Space for Memory and for the Promotion and Defense of Human Rights). The ESMA is emblematic of the horrors committed during the dictatorship and it is the camp to which all others are compared, as it was the most extreme in its cruelty and existed longer than any other camp. Victims held at the ESMA were killed in "death flights," whereby victims were thrown out of navy airplanes into the Atlantic Ocean.

Because of the historic and symbolic importance of the ESMA, I had proposed to the Madres in 2008, a brief study of some of the first tours given there. I was approved to visit on four different occasions. Tours at the ESMA began in January 2008; my first visit in February was only the third tour given, and the site was not yet officially open to the public. At the time, the building that was to hold the *Archivo Nacional de la Memoria* (National Archive of Memory) had not yet been converted. Like all visitors, in order to arrange a visit, I was required to send an email to the organizers and to provide personal identification information, to state how many people were interested in visiting, to list any organizational affiliations, and to explain my desire to visit. The organizers reply with a specific time and date when visitors should arrive for the two-hour tour. The guides are neither direct relatives of the disappeared nor survivors themselves. When

I asked how often tours were offered, the students who serve as the guides, explained the relative infrequency by saying, "We space out the visits to avoid oversaturating ourselves."

The ESMA's Appearance

The military training ground covers approximately forty-two acres, and is composed of thirty-four buildings and is located in a wealthy, residential part of the city. Though it is not in the city center, it sits on one of the major thoroughfares, Avenida del Libertador. The compound is beautiful—uncomfortably so, considering the events that took place there. A relatively short fence of wrought metal surrounds the compound, but does not obscure the buildings, which are still clearly visible from the street. The grounds are very green and peppered with trees. Cars are able to drive through the space on a narrow road that winds around the various buildings. Visitors may not enter all of the buildings; instead they pass the largest buildings, which are located in the center, and spend most of their time in the *Casino de Oficiales* (Officers' Casino), where naval officers tortured victims, ate, and slept.

In the beginning, it was unclear how the former ESMA, run collectively by the national government, the city government of Buenos Aires, and human rights groups, was going to be presented to the public. "[S]ome want a small and simple memorial; others a larger complex that would include a documentation center and human rights academy; others still wish to see the compound razed and replaced with a park" (Williams 2007, 17). Several human rights groups opposed an empty memorialized site, including the Asociación Madres de Plaza de Mayo, whose president, Hebe de Bonafini, was quoted in the left-leaning newspaper *Página/12* on February 1, 2008: "Our disappeared children live; life continues; they beat death. . . . They burned them alive and they couldn't [kill them], they threw them into the river alive, and they couldn't [kill them], they buried them under the highways and they couldn't [kill them]. Our children are not bones; they live on, perpetually reborn, planting themselves seeds in every one of you!" For the Madres, the ESMA should have been a place to demonstrate that the military did not defeat their children, and they felt that that message would be best illustrated by presenting the space not as a place of death—as reflected by the emptiness—but as a place filled with life, humor, happiness, and social activism. The proposal to experience the site as it was left, won in the end. Aside from signs and maps containing survivors' quotes and explanations about how the spaces were used at various stages during and after the dictatorship, the rooms stand empty.[2]

The Tour at the ESMA

The five students who ran the ESMA tours all followed the same narrative, which will offer a point of comparison to how tours were given at D2. The tour I will discuss here took place on February 18, 2008; I chose it because it was the only one I was permitted to record. In general, the focus was on how victims experienced the space, starting from their entry and ending with photographs of the naval officers responsible for the crimes committed there. Visitors learned about the dehumanization process, including the naval officers' use of numbers to replace prisoners' names. The tours began in front of a large map of the naval compound near the front gate, where the guides explain why the ESMA gained its infamous reputation: the death flights, the torture methods, and the highly systematic operation of disappearances at the ESMA that lasted throughout the entire dictatorship.

The tours followed a path that traced the way in which victims entered the compound. As we walked down the main driveway, where cars holding victims in their trunks would pass by a guard post, we were told that there used to be a crossbar that had to be lifted so that cars could enter. The guides explained that they know this is how and where the victims entered, because people who were inside the trunks of cars remembered feeling a speed bump, which remains near the guard post. Although we did not enter the other set of buildings on our right, the tour guide acknowledged them, explaining that they included the infirmary where victims received medical care, including dental care. Keeping victims alive after torture sessions only added to the perverse treatment. The guide said that several survivors recalled their torturers repeating to them that they were the "masters of life and death."

Although there is a functional front entrance to the Officers' Casino, we entered the building from behind just as prisoners once had. "The kidnapped were brought here with shackles already on their feet, with their hands handcuffed; they were walled up and hooded to prevent them from having any sight," the guide said. We entered the hallway; according to testimonies given to international human rights groups by political exiles, survivors recalled seeing high ceilings as they peeked out from behind their blindfolds. The military altered the physical structure of the building specifically to contradict those testimonies, including the installation of a new drop ceiling in this hallway. But as the tour guide pointed out, the new drop ceiling made little architectural sense since it covered the tops of a series of arched windows. When human rights groups hired architects to analyze the structure, this was one of the discrepancies they found.

This altered hallway leads to the lobby of the front entrance. There was once a staircase that victims descended for their initial interrogations, but the floor was filled in to hide this pathway, as the guide pointed out: "One of the modifications that they did was change an entire flight of stairs that went down to the basement. The basement was the first place that they took the captives and they were taken directly through here and inside." The military, however, left a banister piece that would logically lead to a staircase pointed downstairs. The basement is where victims were given a number (or a number and a letter) used by their captors in place of their names. This was the first step of the process of dehumanization that took place at the ESMA.

Before heading upstairs, we were briefly directed to a large conference room off of the lobby, where military officials and civilians held meetings to plan their kidnapping operations. The guide explained that the military collaborated with all sectors of society, not only to conduct the disappearances, but also to hide their crimes from the public: "The task force had three divisions: there was the Intelligence Service part, another part was Operations, and another part was Logistics." By explaining how each of the three groups worked together to track, find, and kidnap their victims, the guide impressed upon the visitors how massive the infrastructure was for disappearing people, and made it clear that far more people were implicated in the crimes than simply uniformed military officers. Doctors, powerful elites, and Catholic priests were some of the military's collaborators.

After exiting the conference room, we stepped outside to another door leading to a short set of stairs, an alternative way to reach the basement.

This staircase was where they gathered people who were about to board one of the death flights: "With regard to the death flights, every Wednesday, around five in the afternoon, there would be announcements for a certain number of detainees who had been preselected." In the basement, the human rights groups installed large maps to illustrate how the space changed multiple times during the dictatorship years to create more torture rooms, slave labor areas, and numerous prison cells. At that point in the tour, the guide explained that while he and his colleagues are the ones giving the tours, the information that they are passing on, is based on survivors' knowledge: "This tour was developed with input from survivors. They were able to enter this space in 2004, but, until that moment, they had not entered into the building since they had been released from the ESMA."

We continued on, walking up the stairs to the top floor. Along the stairwell, there are scratches on the wall—one of the guides said that they were left behind by the victims who were led upstairs blindfolded. The disappeared victims slept in the attic, while their torturers slept on the two floors below. While the attic had virtually no light or ventilation, the naval officers enjoyed a window in each of the building's eighty rooms. At the top of the stairs, the ceilings are lower, the air stuffier, and the space cramped. This is where the victims were kept for days, months, or years. The first two small rooms at the top of the stairs were known as the "pregnancy wing" because it was where prisoners gave birth, handcuffed to the beds. Nothing would suggest that these rooms were used for medical purposes; aside from their extremely small size, there is nothing to distinguish them from any of the other rooms. The guide spoke about the missing grandchildren who the Abuelas are searching for—the children who were born at the ESMA and at other camps and then given away to military families or to their sympathizers.

The rest of the attic is divided into two parts. On the left is where the victims slept on the floor, packed in tightly, like sardines. Thin, metal triangular bars mark the divisions of each cell. The attic walls are slanted, which prevented prisoners from standing up; victims were forced to lie on their mattresses and were prohibited from speaking to each other. There are two tiny windows on each side of the attic floor; it is hard to imagine what the space must have smelled like when it was crammed with the bodies of prisoners suffering from burned flesh, festering wounds, and a general lack of hygiene. Prisoners ate two sandwiches a day and drank *mate cocido* (a bagged version of the traditional grass drink, mate, which is typically served in loose-leaf form).

As we stood in the attic, the guide spoke about one particular woman-prisoner, Norma Arrostito, a leader of the Montoneros who fell in December 1976. Norma, or "Gabi," her nom de guerre, was considered exemplary for withstanding torture, particularly since she was an important figure and a trophy for the military by virtue of her high rank.

When Gabi was imprisoned, the director of the ESMA, Rear Adm. Rubén Jacinto Chamorro (also known as "Delfín" or "Máximo"), would apparently engage in daily conversations with her about politics. This was remarkable as the military often told their female victims that women were incapable of intelligent conversation and were better suited for staying at home. The guide, however, quickly pointed out that not all of the women were guerrillas: "In here there were women other than guerrillas: also housewives, and there were also mothers, others who worked, this one [Arrosito] was. . . ."

At this point, another guide who had been accompanying the tour said, "There is a story, in one part that I read, that it was speculated that Chamorro was. . . ."

"In love," said the first guide, just before the other finished her sentence: "In love with Arrostito." The first guide finished the story, telling us that although Gabi was secluded from other military officers, she received an injection one day and died.

We all paused in silent reflection after hearing the story about Gabi, until the silence was broken when the other guide ushered us back toward the staircase and instructed us to continue walking toward the opposite side of the building in the attic. The guide explained that while one wing was where the captives slept, the other wing was where the military kept stolen goods taken from the victims' homes. And then beyond this storage space was what was once called the "fishbowl." Surrounded by windows, victims who were writers or intellectuals were forced to write fake news reports and propaganda under the watchful eye of the military. The guide drew our attention to the use of euphemisms to describe their actions: "They didn't kidnap people . . . they kidnapped bulk, packages for what they called subversives. Rear Admiral Chamorro, said 'We don't torture human begins; we torture subversives.' Neither were there mass killings; there were transfers. There was no electric shock torture; there was only the machine. There was no asphyxiation; there was the submarine. As we say, they were all euphemisms to make their actions more innocent." Toward the end of the tour, the guides stressed that the people detained at the ESMA were victims—even the ones considered guerrillas:

> The subversive category covers wide sectors of society; it wasn't simply guerrillas. On the same note, I think that by describing them as guerrillas, I am not taking a particular position. I think that all of them were innocent victims. I mean, the word "victim" carries with it, the meaning of innocence. Everything was committed, as we explained before, within the context of a repressive plan by the state, that is, a terrorist state. Therefore the people who were held inside here had no legal rights. They had no legal reason to be here, and they could not present legal cases either. They had none of the procedural guarantees that one would have in a regular penal case.

The tour then ended with a commentary on the ongoing and upcoming trials against the former military officials. The guides said that they wanted to impress upon us that the military personnel who tortured the victims were not, in fact, exceptionally cruel or lunatic, but ordinary people. If considered crazy, then what happened in Argentina seems exceptional, but if instead we regard the military as ordinary, then we must be more vigilant in preventing such cases. In addition, crazy or maniacal torturers may not be fit to stand trial, based on having a mental illness. However, "normal" people who did terrible things, the guides said, can be tried and should stand trial. But without the excuse of writing off the military officials as mentally ill, it is "worse," meaning it is incumbent upon us to understand how it came to be that ordinary people could commit such horrible acts of torture.

We then exited the Officers' Casino and were invited to head toward another building across the compound to view an exhibit presented by Familiares. The display included photographs of known naval officers who worked at the ESMA during the dictatorship (all of them men), as well as newspaper clippings that were published during the dictatorship strung on boards in chronological order. We entered as a group, unguided, and then departed individually.

The Overall Narrative of the ESMA

At the ESMA, the overall tour narrative was focused on how the victims experienced the concentration camp: how they were dehumanized and tortured, and how they lived before their deaths. We learn how the military planned their operations and covered up their crimes—even when international human rights groups investigated. (The military moved the prisoners to a remote location, opened up the ESMA for inspection, and then waited for the inspectors to leave the country before bringing the prisoners back.) The two important additional commentaries made about the prisoners emphasized their exemplary resistance to the military's request for collaboration in the case of Gabi, and their innocence—a quality that the guides applied even to those who were guerrillas. In emphasizing the fact that all ESMA prisoners were tortured and deprived of legal rights, the guides erased the "guilt" of politically involvement. Equating victimhood with innocence, however, obscures the diversity within the category of victim. Thus, the narrative presented at the ESMA is clear: The military engaged in state terrorism. They broke the law and treated other humans in horrific, genocidal ways. The prisoners, no matter who they were, are the victims.

D2 in Córdoba: A Memorial with Ex-Presos

As we will see, the emphasis at D2 was different. D2 had reopened as the home of the Provincial Commission and Archive for Memory in 2006. Although La Perla was arguably the most notorious camp in Córdoba Province, D2 was infamous for the sheer number of people who had passed through there. Prior to the dictatorship, different military governments had detained labor union activists at D2 for several days, and by the time the coup took place, it was already known as the place where interrogation sessions took place.

Because AEPPC members were frequently present at the Archivo either because they had staff positions or were conducting the census there, I spent most of my fieldwork in D2. Gaining access to D2 is simple; with the exception of days designated for staff development, the doors remain open to welcome visitors. Though local schools must prearrange field trips, passersby can simply walk through the entrance. During my time in Córdoba, the physical space changed several times and was in the process of a complete renovation. The exhibits constantly changed, but there was still a blueprint for how the ex-presos gave tours at D2. Before all of the rooms were renovated, I accompanied ex-presos on several official tours and acted as the unofficial translator. The following description is based on the tours given in 2008, by three different AEPPC members who had been detained at D2: Manuel Nieva, Estela Molina, and Juan Carlos Álvarez. For more detailed questions about the experience of giving tours, I drew upon my interview with Juan Carlos.

D2's Appearance

While the ESMA spans an entire former military compound with buildings that once housed officers, D2 is far more modest. The structure is part of a larger historic building, the Cabildo, the seat of colonial government, which sits in the provincial capital's main square. D2 is made up of several small rooms, and it appears today much as it once did—like a small police station. D2 was the place where prisoners were taken most frequently before being transferred to other camps and prisons. Many AEPPC members passed through D2 before being taken elsewhere, and they knew that they were there—despite being blindfolded—because they could hear the church bells of the city's cathedral next door. Other prisoners were able to guess their location by feeling the cobblestone-paved passageway that runs between the Cabildo and the cathedral, known as the Santa Catalina Passage. Unlike the ESMA, which is located in the leafy Buenos Aires neighborhood of Belgrano, D2 is situated in a spot that ensures a very high volume of foot traffic, and its placement in the city center makes it far more accessible for visitors to wander in. D2 is far easier to reach than La Perla, which is tucked away in a soybean field near the air force compound, about 10 kilometers to the west in the outskirts of Córdoba City.

The Tour at D2

Visitors to D2 drop their bags at the front door and are allowed to meander through the space at their own pace. D2 is well staffed with members of human rights groups, students, and young professionals, as well as academics who help conduct archival research and plan events, such as speakers, panels, readings, and art shows. D2's director, Ludmila da Silva Catela, is an anthropologist, and without being an ex-presa, has recognized the importance of ex-presos in helping to create the memorialized space. During my fieldwork, six AEPPC members held staff positions that were specifically designated for them. Four of the ex-presos, who worked as tour guides, were frequently on hand to provide impromptu tours, provided that they were not busy running the office or library, or guiding groups of students from local schools around the space. The two other ex-presos had secretarial and archival responsibilities.

For visitors who sign up for a formal tour of D2, they still do not experience the space exactly as captives had, as they do at the ESMA. For instance, visitors use the main entrance and walk passed the main offices rather than through the gates that prisoners passed through before being interrogated. This way of entering the space has as much to do with the physical building and the absence of a large military compound as it does with the kind of tour given at D2. In the tour that Manuel gave in June of 2008, visitors who were part of a group tour, entered and walked through a narrow hallway until they reached the first available space to stand: the uncovered patio. Once gathered, Manuel drew our attention to a canvas map temporarily strung up on the wall, illustrating the various ways in which the Cabildo was used and how the physical structure changed from the 1500s, to the present day. Standing in front of a map of the Cabildo, Manuel explained that the Cabildo is currently used for multiple purposes, ranging from tourist information to government offices, but that it has long been considered a site of oppression. "Starting as early as the 1700s, the Jesuits, who had colonized Córdoba, used the Cabildo as a place to imprison the indigenous people." He then proceeded to speak about the various military dictatorships in Argentina and the fact that the Cabildo was also used to detain labor union leaders and political dissidents throughout recent history.

Once Manuel established the historical background of D2, he then spoke about broad social and political movements that took place all over the world in the 1960s and 1970s—such as the student uprising in Paris in 1968—and a unified liberation movement in Latin America that was aimed at making the region less dependent on the United States. Manuel circled his hands to emphasize the numerous examples of revolutionary movements and widened his eyes to encourage visitors to offer up their own examples. The ex-presos did this exercise as a way to shift the conversation to the most recent dictatorship in Argentina, and to establish the fact that they know, in no uncertain terms, why they were taken by the military. "We were actors in one of the most important moments in our country's history: the Cordobazo, the movement that brought together students and workers in 1969. We continued to be politically active when the coup took place in 1976, and were disappeared or detained," said Manuel. Instead of speaking about cases of innocent or nonpolitically involved victims, from the start he readily established that he and others were detained for "holding a vision of the world that reflected their values in social equality." Both Manuel and Juan Carlos, the two ex-presos I most often accompanied, shared their belief in a socialist economic model, and explained how that belief led them to join political movements in order to create revolutionary change in Argentina. They also ask the visitors, particularly if they are students, what they think about the current economic situation in Argentina. Usually, after the ex-presos succeed in soliciting some remarks, they then say that they were trying to prevent such social inequalities but were then punished for it. The military came after activists and idealists, as Juan Carlos said, "to prevent them from organizing the *pueblo* (the people)," and to "stifle the liberation movement for Latin America." By tying their personal experiences to the much longer history of oppression in Argentina, the ex-presos stress a pattern of resistance and oppression since the 1500s.

Though the ex-presos do not take visitors along the same route that they followed when they were abducted, and instead orient the tour around the Archivo's exhibitions, they do identify the various spaces they occupied while detained at D2 and recount the types of events that took place in those spaces. Once the introduction is over, the ex-presos point to a set of steps right off the patio. At the bottom is a wall with a gaping hole in the middle, and ragged around the edges. The ex-presos explain that the departing police and military collaborators of the dictatorship constructed the new wall in an attempt to alter the building so as to contradict survivor testimonies. The half–torn down wall is intentional: visitors can both walk through the space as it was originally designed and still view the structural changes that the military constructed.

At the bottom of the stairs, to the left, is a long narrow room where prisoners waited before they were interrogated. When Juan Carlos gave the tour, he explained that he had termed the room the *train station*. Juan Carlos, who remembered being kept in the room, said that the prisoners never bought the train tickets, however, and never knew when the train was arriving. The train metaphor that he adopted, is also a reference to the word *boleto* (ticket), which the military used when a prisoner's number was chosen for a transfer. At the ESMA these transfers were the "death flights." Juan Carlos explained that once a prisoner left the room, the military directed prisoners up the three steps and into one of the various smaller rooms to be interrogated. One of the rooms was up a small staircase, which also acted as the doctor's office, where doctors who collaborated with the military, offered medical opinions on how much torture a person could withstand, and when necessary, treated victims—but only to the point where they were able to be tortured again.

Juan Carlos, along with Manuel and Estela, did not discuss the various torture methods or their own experiences of torture. Instead, the ex-presos simply stated that "the military deprived everyone of their rights and they tortured prisoners during interrogation sessions." Most of the children on the tours, however, ask about torture, according to Juan Carlos. "The challenge for me is that it gets complicated when the kids—who are very young and I am not a teacher—start to ask things like, 'How did they use the electric prod on you?'" (Álvarez, February 2009). I witnessed this on several occasions when I accompanied tours, and was asked about this by foreigners who only spoke English. In response to the question on torture methods, the ex-presos suggest reading *Never Again*, which contains testimonies about the various torture methods used by the military, and simply state that they do not speak about torture.

Before the Archivo was expanded and reopened to the public on March 24, 2009, the ex-presos would continue the tour by ushering visitors into two rooms with special exhibitions. The first one, about

censorship, displayed books that had been prohibited during the dictatorship because their content was deemed subversive, including *The Little
Prince* (1995[1943]) by Antoine de Saint-Exupéry (because of its main character's criticism of societal expectations of adult life and of materialism)
and math books that stress teamwork rather than individual problem
solving. A large photograph of military officials in Córdoba burning books
during the dictatorship hung on the wall. The ex-presos also spoke about
music that was banned, such as folk singer Mercedes Sosa's songs, and
the prohibition against meeting in groups of more than three people. If
parents wanted to hold a birthday party, they first had to receive a permit
from the local police and list all of the names of the guests who would
attend. Showing the breadth and seeming arbitrariness of the list of subversive materials was intended to demonstrate to visitors how easy it was
to be labeled as subversive, since one could be disappeared for owning the
wrong book or record.

For the exhibition in the second room, which has since been expanded,
family members of some disappeared victims in Córdoba created scrap-
books containing photos and letters of the missing persons to show a more
holistic view of the person. Also in the room are some of their belongings:
a necklace, a confirmation dress, a beloved motorcycle, and a few favorite
records. The purpose of this room is to humanize the victims—to show that
these individuals had full, lives, surrounded by friends and family, and to
avoid reducing them simply to torture victims who disappeared.

After visitors have had the opportunity to read through the scrap-
books and to walk through the two rooms on their own, the ex-presos
bring everyone on the tour back together into the patio where they initially began. They conclude the tour by engaging visitors in a discussion
on the political motivations behind the disappearances and why youths
joined revolutionary movements that were sometimes armed. Juan Carlos
and Manuel both discussed the different economic models envisioned by
various leftist groups on one side, and those held by the conservative elite
or the military and its supporters on the other, as a way of explaining why
the conflict erupted in the first place. More time is spent on this topic than
on anything else. Generally, the students I observed at D2 were respectful
and curious during their visits, and spent most of their time absorbing
the information. Similar to older visitors, whose comments I frequently

overheard, the students were shocked to learn that people had once been tortured there. Juan Carlos and Manuel both spoke about their participation in labor unions as the reason for their imprisonment, but noted that others were targeted for working in poor communities, joining political organizations, or holding beliefs that departed from the dictatorship's ideology. "The military sought to crush the revolutionary movements that were gaining momentum and were therefore threatening," said Juan Carlos one afternoon at D2 in April 2009. The lesson, he said, was to become politicized as a way to honor the disappeared and to those who suffered for their ideals. "The greatest defeat was the loss of activist youths," he said. Juan Carlos said he hoped to inspire youths to become politically engaged. Once the conversations end, visitors are allowed to revisit the exhibits before departing the Archivo.

The Overall Narrative at D2

For the ex-presos who work at the Archivo, conducting tours is an extension of their activism. Juan Carlos said that speaking to visitors helped him feel a sense of ownership of the memorialized space, and was a way for him to teach visitors about social movements and repression. He particularly enjoyed being part of a collective with a mission that is both intellectual and personal. "I am in the library and do the guided tours. I visit schools or libraries, along with other compañeros who also share this task. . . . Working here is sometimes painful. It hurts because you lived it with your own flesh. We are talking about our own lives and our own memories. I don't go crazy with every little problem that comes up at the Archivo. I focus on my task. I have to attend to the visitors. I have to search for things from the Archivo. I have to go to the library—all of these things are a form of activism (Ibid.).

For Juan Carlos, working as a tour guide was a way for him to reclaim the same space where he was once held as prisoner. No longer a labor union delegate, he was now teaching youths about the dictatorial past from his point of view as an ex-preso and working to support the Archivo staff in producing and saving archival documents.

A Comparison of the ESMA and D2

At D2, survivors, and specifically the ex-presos, are as visible as the disappeared simply by being present. The guides at the ESMA may thank survivors for their help in developing the tour material, but they are not featured in the space or presented as equally victimized as those who never reappeared. Additionally, because the ex-presos directly address why they were taken, visitors are not left speculating as to why victims were disappeared and whether they deserved to have been taken. At the ESMA, stressing the human rights violations solidifies the victim status of the disappeared. At D2, meanwhile, the human rights questions revolve around competing economic models. Lastly, the staff at D2 consciously chose to present a more complete image of the disappeared as individuals, beyond torture and collaboration with the military.

While guides at both memorial museums described how prisoners moved through the space, where they were kept, and the various purposes of each room, the overall narratives differed significantly in terms of their central messages. While the university students at the ESMA focused on how the dictatorship conducted its systematic disappearances and the types of torture it inflicted upon the victims, the ex-presos provided a much larger historical trajectory when explaining the D2 space in Córdoba. The ex-presos also spoke about the broader social movements going on throughout the world in the 1960s and 1970s, and how this historical and cultural context shaped the political motivations behind their abductions and the enduring social impacts of the dictatorship's economic policies. At the ESMA, the guides shared stories about specific disappeared victims,[3] whereas at D2, the ex-presos sought to destabilize the widely circulated image of the innocent victim by explicitly stating that they know why they were targeted. Students at the ESMA spoke about the torture methods and the way in which the military coordinated disappearances.

At the ESMA, the tour narrative could be summed up as one of torture and victimization; the message for visitors is that they must work to prevent future atrocities, and that the former military officials should be put on trial. Meanwhile at D2, the tour narrative revolves around the theme of social movements and state oppression. The message the ex-presos try to convey is that democracy must be supported in order to allow people to be as politically engaged as possible—even when that democratic freedom is threatening to those who wield power.

While the ex-presos at D2 do not directly address the collaborator question, by virtue of speaking about their participation in social movements, they introduce a grayer landscape than if they spoke only about being victims of gross human rights violations, such as torture and forced disappearance. Ex-presos explain how the military disappeared victims, and then speak about their roles as activists. The dual presence of the disappeared and survivors increases the complexity of the past, and highlights the fact—without explicitly stating it—that not all victims were guilty of collaboration and not all were righteous in their commitment to the collective political project. As Daniel, a former political prisoner, explained, "Some compañeros who broke were still killed, and those who remained in solidarity also disappeared."

Yet not all victims were treated the same socially and legally after the dictatorship. (How the social and legal treatment of ex-presos differed will be further explored in chapter 4.) Even as ex-presos dispute the dichotomy between desaparecidos and survivors, they also reinforce the division in many ways themselves. In a personal conversation shortly before I left in June 2009, Juan Carlos said, "The best among us disappeared." Even the ex-presos view death as the ultimate sacrifice. But Juan Carlos and his compañeros seek to distance themselves from the accusation that they were traitors by distinguishing themselves from those who collaborated in prison, even if those "traitors" were few and far in between. This distinction, rather than moving away from thinking in absolutes, reinforces the good versus bad mentality that characterizes the disappeared versus survivor dichotomy that has negatively harmed the ex-presos.

Comparing the two memorial museums may raise questions more than it provides answers. Though I would argue that the presence of survivors at sites elevates their victim status to equal that of the disappeared, the reliance upon survivors to give tours is a risky move because they are aging and beginning to pass away. Who will fill this gap? Does the fact that the tours at the ESMA emphasize the disappeared and the human rights violations they suffered reflect an enduring belief that the disappeared were not only more victimized than the survivors for having died, but also more heroic for having given their lives over to the revolutionary cause?

Does it matter if the survivor conducting the tours was a collaborator or not? These questions may not be answerable, but perhaps the presence of survivors may force both visitors and the Argentine public to recognize the diversity of victims and to question our tendency to look at the past in absolutes.

In Buenos Aires, the AEDD had declined to be involved with the creation of the ESMA as a memorialized space, believing that it was a departure from their overall mission of political activism (Van Drunen 2010). Not all survivors see involvement with these spaces of memory as part of their activism. The AEPPC members, in contrast, believe that survivors should be present at the ESMA, and seek to be on the staff at memorial museums in Córdoba, in part because they believe their voices have not yet been heard. The ex-presos conducting tours at D2 demand that visitors think about the roles of armed revolutionary groups and the state's response to them. If, as I suggest, the dual presence of the disappeared in the imaginary and the survivors in situ, helps to keep the gray area in the minds of visitors and educators, then the ability to be present at memorial museums offers ex-presos a chance to push back against accusations that they betrayed their compañeros. Being present at memorial museums provides the ex-presos with a platform from which to make the case that democratic activism—not only trials—are an appropriate response to the human rights violations of the past.

4

Solidarity and Resistance in Prison

Former political prisoners do not want to talk about torture. In 2008, a group of volunteer psychologists briefly presented themselves at one of AEPPC's weekly meetings, offering free therapeutic services to the ex-presos in case the recent trial against former military officials unearthed old memories or created new challenges. It had been nearly three decades since the ex-presos were released from prison, and no one took them up on their offer. As AEPPC member Rosa Noto said in May 2008, after a weekly meeting, "All [psychologists] want to know about is how we were tortured, or if they can conduct a study about our lives as [torture] victims, or give us treatment." "We have gone for so long without any help," said another AEPPC member, Américo Aspitia, during a personal conversation in April 2009. Many ex-presos believed that they had already carried on with their lives without having sought out psychological help; the idea of a therapist was seen by many as coming too late. Instead, the AEPPC membership was most interested in recalling memories of resistance and solidarity—about how political prisoners survived and held close their activist identities. "The prison guards would tell you that you had three ways of leaving prison: *loco* (crazy), *puto* (fucked), or *quebrado* (broken)," said AEPPC member Atilio Basso (Basso, October 2008). Ex-presos told stories that proved the military wrong; they had remained steadfast in their activist ideals even in prison and despite torture.

In public venues, the AEPPC president, Sara Liliana Waitman, would argue that political prisoners suffered and continued to suffer the consequences of torture and exposure to harsh prison conditions, and that the state should financially compensate them for these harms and injuries. In their oral history archive interviews, however, most AEPPC members denied that they were seriously impaired either psychologically or physically. This contradiction—stating for a historical record that there was no continued suffering while simultaneously lobbying state senators for reparations to compensate for that suffering—presented a challenge for me. What did it mean if, when it suited them, the ex-presos said that they and their compañeros were still feeling the negative effects of torture and prison conditions—and then, when they felt they were speaking for posterity, they stated the exact opposite?

In this chapter, I argue that this contradiction of being simultaneously affected and not affected by torture and degrading prison conditions is a reflection of the ex-presos' desire to be remembered for their activism rather than for having been tortured. Even though they were, in fact, tortured and forced to live in degrading prison conditions, the ex-presos spent their time in memorial museums, writing and producing film projects, and participating in oral history archive interviews focusing on how they broke the rules and expressed solidarity with one another in prison. By presenting stories that illustrate the themes of solidarity and resistance, I suggest that the ex-presos demonstrate their resilience as ideologically committed resisters whom the military tried—and failed—to break down with its torture methods.

I am not a clinician. However, I noticed that, during AEPPC meetings, members frequently spoke about how they all continued to be impacted by their time in prison. Emotions at these meetings often ran high, and many ex-presos displayed some *pós-trauma* (posttrauma, the shorthand they used for posttraumatic stress syndrome [PTSD]). Some póstrauma symptoms that I observed and were discussed by the ex-presos about themselves were depression, aggression, and paranoia (see Stover and Nightingale 1985). Several ex-presos mentioned these behaviors and emotions outside of meetings, during personal conversations in the street, or in coffee shops. At the first few meetings I attended, several members expressed their embarrassment for "behaving badly" in front of an American anthropologist, but as I became a constant fixture and compañera, there was no holding back. I witnessed many heated arguments: papers were slammed on tables, personal insults were shouted, and certain members were prone to storm out of meetings. I also witnessed black humor and kindness: people made jokes in the middle of debates and members shared mate and bread. I also witnessed several times when a member would cry out of frustration or anger, and others would respond by admitting to mutual feelings of pós-trauma. For example, once, after a compañero broke down and cried while speaking, another member announced that they all needed therapy. Among the group of about forty-five regular attending members, only about four compañeros were known to receive some form of group therapy. While the ex-presos may not actively pursue therapy, it is highly likely that some or all of them suffer from trauma related to their time in prisons and in concentration camps.

Outside of the meetings, ex-presos would frequently speak about what happened to them when they were imprisoned, or how the torture they underwent in prison continued to haunt them. For instance, I had lunch with a couple of ex-presos during a session break at the trial against former army gen. Luciano Benjamín Menéndez. At one point in the meal, in the course of an otherwise ordinary conversation, "Cynthia"[1] told me that she had difficulty having sex with her husband because of the multiple rapes she endured as a prisoner in a concentration camp. Conversations like the one I had with Cynthia happened frequently, particularly during social gatherings—during the *merienda* (mid-afternoon meal) of mate and pastries, or at weekend barbecues. Once, after a weekly AEPPC meeting, members gathered at a corner café, and the conversation that night turned from local current events to a report that one ex-preso, who was not part of the AEPPC, was suffering from mental health problems and had taken to sleeping in a closet. Several compañeros nodded knowingly. In response, a couple of ex-presos recalled their own prison cells, which were dark, cramped, and windowless. Others said that they felt lucky to have had a small hole or even a tiny window in their prison cells. Comparing notes, the ex-presos would indulge in black humor and make light of their harrowing living conditions in prison. Stories seeped out in the most unexpected situations, and they revealed to me how enduring the effects were and how dark moments surfaced unevenly at different times.

Although I witnessed and heard how the ex-presos and their compañeros suffered from what happened to them in the past, I was also conscientious about taking them at their word, particularly considering the fact that they knew I was recording their stories as an ethnographer. The ex-presos' desire to distance themselves from torture stories may be in response to the great interest in, and literature written on, torture victims from South America in the 1980s (Stover and Nightingale 1985; Suárez-Orozco 2004; Weschler 1990). The international human rights movement had focused heavily on the denouncement of torture as its primary intervention in the state violence that took over Latin America in the 1970s and 1980s (see Moyn 2010, 147). The AEPPC members want the state to pay them financial reparations for having been tortured, but they also want, particularly as they age, to be remembered for their activism and not just for their victimization.

Interrogation and Torture Methods

Because the ex-presos avoid relating stories about their experiences of torture, this book does not discuss torture and its specific aftereffects extensively. However, understanding how the military treated the ex-presos helps explain why they are seen as victims, and why the AEPPC is lobbying for economic compensation for what happened to them in prison. I will summarize how ex-presos generally experienced interrogations in Córdoba before turning to their memories of solidarity and resistance.

Perhaps what most defined state terrorism during the dictatorship was the abduction of political dissidents and the violence committed against them in interrogation sessions. When ex-presos fell, they were almost always blindfolded before being forced into cars and taken to secret torture camps. In Córdoba, this sensory deprivation worked to disorient captives before they were taken to D2, which was an "intake" center as it was often the first place prisoners were taken to before being transferred somewhere else, or straight to concentration camps, such as La Perla. Prisoners at both places were subjected to interrogation sessions that involved torture. Using metal, rubber, and wooden truncheons, the military or police would beat prisoners until they were bloodied and bruised. In some cases, prisoners were left with partial disabilities, broken bones, ruptured kidneys, and, for some pregnant female prisoners, spontaneous miscarriage (IACHR 1980). The most frequently used torture technique was the *picana*, an electric prod that delivered high-voltage shocks to the body. Interrogators applied the picana to their victims' genitals and breasts, to their temples, hands, legs, and feet, as well as to sensitive areas such as the gums and eyes. Torturers also used a spoon-like tool to pass electric shocks to the fetuses of pregnant prisoners. To intensify the electric currents, the interrogators would tie prisoners to metal bed frames and pour water over them, which would cause the prisoner's flesh to burn at every point of contact with the metal. The military called this a *parilla,* or "grill"—the kind that Argentines use to prepare weekend barbecues. In addition to the picana, many captives also endured the *submarino,* which literally translates to "submarine" and refers to a method of torture in which the victim's head is repeatedly pushed underwater and is intended to simulate the feeling of drowning. For many victims, the worst part was the putrid water, or being able to taste the previous victims' mouths in the water. When they were not being tortured, prisoners were kept in inhumane conditions, starved, denied permission to go to the bathroom, and subjected to sexual abuse. Psychological forms of torture were used throughout imprisonment: in some cases, prisoners' children would be kidnapped and forced to witness the torture sessions in order to inflict emotional pain onto their parents.

The dictatorship's prisoners were not only tortured in secret concentration camps; even when they were placed in regular prisons, the military treated political prisoners more harshly than regular prisoners. Guards regularly punished political prisoners and revoked standard rights without much rationale or logic in order to continually frustrate, confuse, and threaten prisoners. For example, guards would place prisoners in solitary confinement for speaking when they had, in fact, been silent. Political prisoners were frequently removed from their prison cells for interrogation sessions, and at the beginning of the dictatorship, some were taken out and executed. Placed in small, individual cells without windows, prisoners had restricted mobility. I include some excerpts from interviews with two political prisoners on their personal experiences in the camps and prisons.

María del Carmen "Carmencita" Pérez

Carmen, nicknamed "Carmencita," was fifty-three years old at the time I interviewed her in her home for the oral history archive. We were both on the AEPPC's editorial committee for the group's self-published volume of testimonies, *Eslabones*, and often saw each other at meetings, social gatherings, and rallies. Carmen is a widow; her husband, with whom she had a son, died from the aftereffects of torture to the brain. The military had kidnapped Carmencita on April 13, 1978, when she was twenty-three years old, for being a member of the Montoneros. Immediately after her abduction, the military took her to La Perla, where she was held for three months, until July 18, 1978.

CARMENCITA: When they tortured you with electric shock, they never took you to the shower immediately after—unless they had passed the current through you only once. But not if they used the electric prod a lot, because the water—the electric currents stay in the body for several days.

REBEKAH: You mean the picana?

CARMENCITA: Right, the picana is the electric prod and that electric current stays inside you. Imagine that you touched a half-exposed cable while you're fixing something at home. It shocks you. You shouldn't get wet. That is, you have to wait at least a day or two. The more electric current, the longer you have to wait before getting wet. I think I was there [in La Perla] for more than a week. They tortured me on the first day with the picana. They applied it to my entire body, stomach, and mouth. And then they didn't do it again. The next day I was in bad shape because of the multiple blows I took to my kidneys and back. I don't even remember if I had bruises, because I never even looked. I had a lot of infections, in the ears especially, because they had dunked my head in the dirty water bin,[2] and because of the general lack of hygiene—you couldn't clean yourself! I lost hearing in my right ear. (Pérez, August 2008)

After being transferred several times to other camps and prisons, Carmencita was eventually released on December 24, 1982.

Norma Peralta

Norma and I became friends after spending time together during a trip to Buenos Aires for a pro-government rally on July 15, 2008. At the time

I interviewed Norma, she was fifty-six years old and had never given her testimony before. We conducted the interview in the patio of the office of Familiares, during her break from administering the census of political prisoners in Córdoba Province. The child of a taxi driver and a nurse, Norma came from a middle-class family. She started medical school in 1972, and, after attending various rallies for several different political causes, she became politically active and joined the PRT in 1973. The military abducted Norma and her then-husband "Greg"[3] in 1975, although they had gone underground in an attempt to escape. Before taking them to a torture camp, the *patota* (gang) beat them for a few hours, blindfolded them, and then took them to the center of police intelligence:

> They took us to D2, and it was a crazy place: the screams, the sounds of the constant blows of multiple fists everywhere. I think they had beaten me for two straight days. They did the submarine on me. Throughout my time there, I stuck to my decision to never ask permission to go to the bathroom. Instead, I just went on myself, on top of everything else, because. . . . [pause] I was already completely filthy. At one point, they took me to the head authority and I was naked. I don't remember if they stripped me naked or if I undressed myself. I was so dirty and I smelled really awful. The guy in charge said: "Take this filthy, skinny girl away from me; she smells bad." I thought to myself, "Great!" I was very happy to have been taken away. (Peralta, October 2008)

Norma's strategy was itself a form of resistance; by making herself revolting, she managed to avoid being further interrogated or sexually assaulted by the commanding officer:

> They were also severely beating my husband, but after awhile, I could no longer tell who was being hit because there were noises everywhere around me, and it felt like you were surrounded by the incessant screaming. At one point they took me upstairs to see the doctor so that he could determine if I was able to endure more torture. He said, "Yes, she can stay put. . . ." After that, they didn't take me down to be tortured again. The following day, or it must have been the eighteenth, I don't know what day it was, but Charlie

> Moore—who was supposedly in PRT but acted as a collaborator and
> committed torture—took me to the bathroom, removed my blind-
> fold, and told me not to look at him. He said I was the stupid one
> in the end because I was the idiot for being in a relationship with a
> male whore, because my compañero had photos of Mao Zedong, of
> Che Guevara in the apartment. He was screaming at me—he was a
> complete monster. I remember Charlie Moore being a monster, as
> being completely crazy. (Ibid.)

A doctor examined her, and assessed that she could not withstand more
torture. In accordance with the doctor's recommendation, it was not until
a few days later that Norma was tortured again by Carlos Raimundo "Charlie" Moore.[4]

Norma had been detained with a large volume of people in D2, and as a
result, the police and military personnel debated what to do with all of the
captives within earshot of them. She recalled this moment of not knowing
whether she was going to be executed or taken to another location:

> "Let's kill them all," some of the guards said. But other guards said:
> "No, we should take them to jail." The ones who thought we should go
> to jail won. We were then loaded onto a bus on the Santa Catalina Pas-
> sage, because I remember feeling the stones beneath my feet. We were
> still blindfolded, but once they threw us inside the truck, we took
> off our hoods and saw what a mess we were all in. There were a
> lot of beaten-up people. There was one compañera who had just
> had a baby, and I remember her face was all bruised and all over
> her body. Her husband, too, was all beaten and bruised. I remember
> them, and the fact that there were many of us in the back of the
> truck. They took all of us to the jail, to UP1. (Ibid.)

However, the military did not kill everyone, and some prisoners made it
to the next destination: sometimes another torture camp and other times
a regular prison. The liminal period before a prisoner arrived at his or her
destination, however, was fraught with uncertainty and fear.

Impact of Torture

The multiple beatings and various torture techniques that prisoners were exposed to during their interrogation sessions left behind serious long-term physical and psychological effects. AEPPC member Juan Carlos Álvarez, who was imprisoned for eight and half years for being part of a labor union and a Montonero, had his head beaten repeatedly—torturers would clap down on both his ears simultaneously in a torture technique called the "telephone." The repeated blows to his head caused Juan Carlos to lose hearing in one ear, and to experience a constant buzzing sound in the other. He also suffers from severe migraines and nausea, the latter symptom a result of impaired balance, which comes in turn from his uneven sense of hearing. I learned about his condition in one of my first interactions with him. While waiting for a protest march for labor rights to start, Juan Carlos told me that he suffered from ear problems. When I asked him if he had an ear infection, he shook his head and then mimed hitting the sides of his head. I immediately knew that he was speaking of torture. Every so often Juan Carlos would stay at home because of severe migraines caused from the constant buzzing, imbalance, and dizziness.

For others, the consequences were even more severe. AEPPC member María Mercedes "Chicha" Aranguren de Schreurer[5] spoke to me about her late husband, Carlos Enrique Schreurer, who was held prisoner in La Perla and who later died from the injuries he sustained during interrogation sessions. Chicha's husband was an activist in the Peronist Youth organization through his university's student council. In 1971, the military government imprisoned him twice, but he was eventually released. At the time of the military coup in 1976, Carlos was working for Córdoba's municipal government. In November of that year, he was fired, and the military went looking for him at his home. He was abducted and disappeared to La Perla, where he remained until May 1977. This was a particularly long period of time to be kept at a torture camp; at that early stage of the dictatorial rule, most prisoners were either executed within weeks of their arrival or transferred to other camps and prisons. Chicha met Carlos after his release from La Perla.

Around 1990, Carlos began to suffer from memory loss, and his condition continued to deteriorate until he lost all mobility, eventually degenerating into a vegetative state. Chicha explained that the doctors attributed his brain damage to the multiple blows he took to the head when he was held at La Perla. Before his death in 2004, he was bedridden for a decade; he spent the first year of that decade in the hospital. When Carlos first became ill, Chicha worked three jobs—her main employment was teaching disabled children—in order to support her husband's medical needs and to provide for their three children. However, after a couple of years, without government assistance to help people like Carlos, Chicha quit her three jobs to take care of him. She instead cleaned offices in two-hour shifts, three times a day. Between these times, she cared for her husband and raised her children, one of whom suffered from Crohn's disease.

In addition to the lack of government support, Chicha also lacked social support because of the broader societal distrust of former political prisoners. While most of Chicha's friends and neighbors shunned her, believing that her husband must have done something to deserve his imprisonment at La Perla, there were a few exceptions. Chicha's sister-in-law, whose brother was disappeared with his wife and child,[6] was supportive. And while Chicha was taking care of her rapidly deteriorating husband, she found a friend in Carmencita, the ex-presa whose description of her own experience at La Perla was just quoted. Like Carlos, Carmencita's husband was suffering from severe psychological and neurological damage. Carmencita and Chicha met at the headquarters of Familiares in 2001, before the AEPPC formed. Chicha said that Carmencita helped her spiritually, and she felt that she understood her. Together with three other ex-presas whose husbands also suffered from severe health problems related to imprisonment, Chicha conducted an informal health survey of political prisoners in Córdoba in the early 2000s. Her husband's case was extreme, Chicha said, but it was not unique: "There are other people who were detained in clandestine centers who were confined to a bed like my husband. The vast majority had been severely tortured" (Aranguren de Scheurer, September 2008).

Not all ex-presos' health problems stem directly from having undergone specific torture techniques; others come from living in degrading conditions that impacted their psychological and physical well-being. The purpose of putting prisoners in horrific conditions was to erode their sense of humanity and individuality: "This very harsh system aggravated any diseases already suffered prior to abduction and brought on others as a result of burns, bleeding and infection: many women had their menstrual cycles interrupted because of the conditions. These were imposed with the aim of destroying the individual identity of the prisoners, this being an essential objective of the methodology we have been analyzing" (CONADEP 1986 [1984], 65). The military treated prisoners like animals, and these living conditions contributed to the dehumanization process. Consider the way in which prisoners at La Perla were forced to eat, as described by Carmencita:

> You pass the first few days expecting utensils to eat with, like a fork and a knife. And they tell you, "Lift up the blindfold to eat," and there you are waiting for them to hand over some utensils but they never do. They came up to me with the food and then took it away and said, "Why didn't you eat?" And when I said I was waiting for a spoon, the guard told everyone, "There is not a single spoon for anyone here." There was nothing but your hands to eat the noodles, to eat the stew, to eat the soup. And they came around with a pot that was the size of an oval dish about fifteen or twenty centimeters wide and about twenty-eight or thirty centimeters [11-12 inches] long, made out of aluminum and with an army logo on it. (Pérez, August 2008)

And the food prisoners were served was insufficient, as documented in *Never Again*: "The infrequency and inferiority of meals constituted another form of torment. Prisoners were fed—depending on the center—once or twice a day, but on many occasions several days went by when they were given no food at all. At other times they were given water with flour or raw offal. In general, rations were barely enough, and anybody who tried to give some to another person in a worse state than themselves, was severely punished. Solidarity was forbidden" (CONADEP 1986[1984], 64). Ex-presos believe that many of their health problems were caused by severe malnutrition and by the inferior quality of food.

AEPPC member Ovidio Ramón Ferreyra, or "Pajarito," which translates to "little bird"—a nickname he earned for singing in his cell during the seven years he spent in prison—claimed that being forced to shower under cold water was actually a form of torture. The cold showers, which prisoners were sometimes forced to take four times a day, were not about cleanliness. The cold showers turned what should have been a normal activity into an act of torture that they believed to have weakened their bodies: "In the beginning they almost never took us to bathe, or to the patio, or even allowed us to speak. But later they took us to shower, but there was only freezing water, because, more than a matter of hygiene, it was a form of torture that they wanted to inflict upon us. It was really cold and when the water fell it felt like needles puncturing, like a splinter that broke through the skin" (Ferreyra, October 2008). Similarly, Sara Liliana Waitman blamed the overall cold temperatures for bone deterioration: "We didn't have any heat and the cells were freezing. The hallway was freezing. There was no sun—all of these factors caused wear and tear on the bones" (Waitman, September 2008). Several ex-presos recalled being without proper clothes and blankets in the winter. For Viviana "Viva" Vergara, the poor diet, lack of access to medical and dental care, and cramped cell all contributed to her overall poor physical condition:

> I got out of prison and I immediately had to get glasses, or at the very least had to use reading glasses. Then I developed chronic gastritis that I still suffer from because of all of the fat that I ate while I was a prisoner. The majority came out [of prison] with some kind of gastritis. We ate a lot of fat in prison, fat from lamb, from pork—it was fat constantly . . . I never went to the dentist when I was in prison since they didn't use anesthesia. They don't wait for the anesthesia to take effect and they don't ask you if it does. Once, I wanted them to fix a tooth and I didn't get any anesthesia and I had to grab the dentist's arm. I never went back again to the dentist, and ended up losing most of my molars. I also have back problems because the bunk beds were right on top of one another and they pressed down on us when we sat underneath them. We would usually gather below the bed to read letters, but then had spine-related problems. (Vergara, August, 2008)

Most of the ex-presos trace their dental and back problems to the degrading prison conditions they endured for years, as a result of either lack of access to care or the fact that they were forced to live in cramped living quarters and to subsist on whatever was given to them.

For some ex-presos, the overall experience of having been tortured and imprisoned caused psychological problems. In her recorded interview, I asked AEPPC member Élida "Ely" Eichenberger about the time I first learned about her inability to recall the names of compañeros:

> Because it took so much willpower to not recall names, my psychologist, or rather my psychiatrist, termed what I have as *reactive amnesia*. You ask me a question and it's a question with an answer that I definitely know but I can't respond. If you ask me something ordinary like, "What is the name of your grandson?" I think, "My grandson? No! I don't know his name." They asked me about people in prison and I had to protect them. Because of the energy I put into not giving up information during the torture sessions, even when I was getting electric shock torture. When you ask me a question today, I still make myself go blank. I have to wait a little bit before answering, and after awhile, my memory returns. They call this reactive amnesia; it's a consequence of torture. (Eichenberger, October 2008)

Ely recalled denying all of the accusations that the military made and refusing to confirm any information when she was tortured. When asked for names, she responded by going blank, forcing herself to forget, because if she remembered, then she could risk giving up a name. So strong was her mental reformulation, however, that this strategy stayed with her long after she was released from prison. Because her grandson is someone who she has to protect, she automatically refuses to tell others his name, although she is no longer being tortured and she lives under a democratic Argentina. Ely told me that her problem with names was common among other compañeros for the same reason.

While Ely had a specific response to a particular aspect of the interrogations, AEPPC member Américo Aspitia reported suffering schizophrenia since 1994, after his time in prison. Américo said it took him several years to accept his mental illness because he "was in denial." "I appeared normal, but in fact, I was just trying to deal with it on my own, and I kept it from my family, from my own children. I was generally fine but there were moments, or days, when I'd go into my workshop and not reappear for a day. I didn't want to be around anyone because I didn't feel good, or because I was feeling very aggressive" (Aspitia, April 2009). When Américo finally consulted a doctor after experiencing panic attacks and fainting, he was told that he "didn't have anything." In reaction, Américo said, "How dare you say that to me? I'm not fine—you son of a bitch!" He saw himself as "a walking, ticking bomb" (Ibid.). For instance, Américo remembered the time when he was sharing a cup of coffee at a bakery with his wife when someone placed his hands on his shoulders. Thinking that he was being kidnapped again, Americo nearly threw the man to the floor, only to realize it was a friend attempting to greet him. His illness also affected his wife: "At night when I was sleeping, my wife would sometimes be crying next to me. She'd wake up crying because I had jabbed her hard with my elbow or kicked her. She insisted that we go see a psychologist to see if I was crazy—I wasn't crazy" (Ibid.). Even though Américo was in denial, his family knew that they had to be careful around him: "They knew that when I reached a certain point, I couldn't control myself. They already knew this about me. This was one of the repercussions of having been a prisoner. One time my grandchildren gave me a little whistle from the carnival as a gift, and I went crazy when it blew. I got really irritated, because the whistle reminded me of having to follow orders in prison. When I heard the whistle, I would have to lie down because it was like a cloud came over me. Everyone around me just watched because they didn't know what to do" (Ibid.). Américo did not receive any psychological help because he felt like "there were no psychologists for us," a sentiment he shared with other ex-presos who failed to find a therapist who they felt could truly understand their struggles.

For AEPPC member Ester Cabral, even a seemingly innocuous smell triggered an extreme reaction. In a personal conversation on July 20, 2008, Ester remembered reacting harshly toward a boy on the street who attempted to sell her perfume: "The owner of a nearby kiosk saw what happened and told me not to be so hard on the kid because he was just trying to make a living." Upon reflection, Ester realized that cologne reminded her of her torturer. "While I couldn't see him through my blindfold, I still remember the stench of his heavy cologne."

During my own fieldwork, I witnessed how ordinary events triggered traumatic reactions in self-defense. For instance, I remember standing and chatting with three ex-presas near the main town square when a teenage boy approached one of the women, "Pamela,"[7] from behind to ask for money. I watched Pamela freeze and her body immediately tightened. She put her hand to her chest and began to breathe harder and faster. Later, Pamela told me that her heart was beating fast and that she was having a panic attack. She also explained that this was how she was kidnapped—they came up to her from behind and put a knife to her. A few days later, she told me that she was still shaken from the emotions and memories that resurfaced as a result of the boy's approach from behind, not unlike what had happened to Américo. While there was nothing particularly diagnosable or life-threatening in this instance, this is but one illustration of how ex-presos live with memories of past violence.

Beyond specific instances in which ex-presos felt the past upon them, many spoke in personal conversations about one another's problems with depression and difficulty with sleeping. AEPPC member Fidel "Antonio" Alcázar, who was imprisoned for four years and eight months for being a leftist sympathizer, believed that the biggest impact on his life was his unrelenting desire for justice: "I held a lot of anger toward the military—and I think that the trial against [former gen.] Menéndez gave me some relief. The trials against all former military officials are the only solace for the lack of a sense of peace after all that has happened to us. I don't see it as vengeance but as justice, because it's about upholding the laws in a country. They committed crimes against humanity, because they didn't respect the law. Instead of bringing someone to trial, they killed and tortured people indiscriminately" (Alcázar, October 2008).

For Antonio, the problem that persisted after his release had less to do with his own physical body and more with his anger at the absence of any official recognition that he had been wronged. Elsewhere in his interview, Antonio said that the sentencing of those who were responsible for his torture and imprisonment gave him a sense of lightness—as he put it, his spirit was alleviated by the trials. Antonio's feelings carry serious implications for arguments in favor of trials in postwar or post–mass violence settings, particularly in places where truth commissions are created in place of trials.

The notion that justice may alleviate PTSD is a contested one. In a public lecture given at the University of California, Los Angeles, on March 8, 2010, Ana Deutsch, one of the cofounders of the Los Angeles–based Program for Torture Victims, argued that torture leaves individuals feeling powerless and that the absence of justice is related to posttraumatic stress disorder. However, Dianna Ortiz, an American nun who was tortured in 1989, by the military for working with an indigenous community in Guatemala and who later founded the organization, Torture Abolition and Survivor Support Coalition, informed me in 2008, that many survivors of torture she met had expected to feel relief after justice, but found themselves feeling dissatisfied instead. No reparation can fully compensate for what happened to them, but the AEPPC still desires justice, both legal and symbolic.

"Not all suffered from what had happened to them in prison with the same intensity afterward," said AEPPC member Atilio Basso (October 2008). Atilio, after having been imprisoned for four and a half years for his PRT activities, admitted to having problems with his joints, vision, and teeth because of his time in prison. Yet he did not feel that he had suffered psychologically as others had, with the exception of feeling melancholy from time to time at the memory of his disappeared compañeros. In fact, Atilio believed that he was one of the lucky ones who had come out relatively unscathed. But he was committed as an AEPPC member to finding a way to give practical relief to his compañeros who were suffering intensely from the aftereffects of torture and their traumatic abductions. On March 16, 2010, not long after I returned to the United States, Atilio died from heart failure. His compañeros believe that his heart condition was a result of having been tortured and having lived under tremendous stress in prison.

Bifurcated Identity

In order to get any depth of insight into the dynamics of being both a victim and a political agent, I have devoted half of this chapter to establishing the context of extreme violence and terror in which memories of resistance and solidarity are situated. While ex-presos did not want to tell stories of torture at the point when I met them, I found it necessary to establish what happened in camps and in prisons in order to understand the tension between the bifurcated identities of sufferer and activist that ex-presos embody. Ex-presos in Argentina asked for reparations on the basis of their torture victim status and then stated in oral history interviews that they came out of prison relatively unharmed. This bifurcated identity, however, was not an outright contradiction. Instead, this simultaneous acknowledgment and denial was a reflection of the ex-presos' reality: they were affected by past violence, but they emerged from their ordeal as victors. Ex-presos would explain in educational venues (tours, panels, and speaking engagements) that the military tried to destroy them as people, using torture and imprisonment to instill enough fear to prevent them from ever wanting to engage in any future political activities. But ex-presos want those listening to them to understand that they never gave up on their political commitments, even in prison. In their oral history interviews, which they treated as permanent records of their past, the ex-presos spoke about their political awakenings, the history of social movements, their time in detention, and their ability to continue with political activities in the AEPPC. By suggesting that—despite all that they endured—they are not "crazy, fucked, or broken," the ex-presos are also defiantly stating that the military did not succeed in silencing them, even with their brutal methods.

The ex-presos want recognition that they were victimized, but they do not want stories of torture to veer into pornography of violence. For example, Iain Guest's (1990) otherwise exemplary book, *Behind the Disappearances: Argentina's Dirty War against Human Rights and the United Nations*, which was written based on confidential documents and memoranda, contains several descriptions of torture that are typical of reports on the victims of Argentina's most recent dictatorship, including this one:

> Nine doctors were seen in the hospital by detainees. One, who had been given the macabre name of "Mengele," was present as Ana María Martí was stripped and tied to the steel bed frame. She watched, dazed, as Caroline was attached to a box on a table. The insect's antennae were throbbing and dancing with the current, its jaws open. They closed on the steel frame. Then came the agony, unspeakable agony, as the insect moved hungrily over her body, probing, spitting and spluttering while Antonio Pernía's grin hovered above.
>
> It was unhurried and methodical. If the victim was a woman they went for the breasts, vagina, anus. If a man, they favored genitals, tongue, neck. The aim was to cause disorientation as much as pain.

Sometimes victims twitched so uncontrollably that they shattered their own arms and legs. Patrick Rice, an Irish priest who had also worked in slums and was detained for several days, recalls watching his flesh sizzle. What he most remembers is the smell. It was like bacon. (Guest 1990, 41)

These descriptions, which were not written long after the fall of the dictatorship, were powerful in revealing the extent to which the military committed human rights abuses. The dramatization and attention to detail—what the burning flesh smelled like, the pace at which the torturers passed electric currents through victims' bodies, and the smiles that the torturers wore while witnessing pain—depict for readers the reality of what happened at the hundreds of secret detention camps. Human rights organizations convey the severity of the repression by including survivors' testimonies and detailed descriptions of torture methods in their reports (Amnesty International 1979; IACHR 1980). Amnesty International got its start by waging international campaigns against torture and focusing on individual cases of political prisoners (Keys 2012, 202); the brutality of torture is indisputable. Similarly, the 1984 truth commission report, *Never Again*, drew upon torture survivor testimonies and eyewitness accounts from families of the disappeared.

Without a doubt, there is a time and a place to document torture and prison conditions, and documentation is critical in incriminating perpetrators. Ex-presos are often expected to speak about torture when giving testimony for trials, teaching groups of schoolchildren about the recent past, or meeting with international human rights representatives. While they acknowledge that they suffered from torture, they desire a more positive picture of themselves in history. When we restrict the survivors' narrative to accounts of human rights abuses like these, we fail to see not only the broader context of their suffering, but also how the survivors want their time in prison to be remembered. The ex-presos reminded one another in meetings that their writing projects, speaking engagements, and memorials were about recalling their *solidaridad* (solidarity) and *resistencia* (resistance)—before, during, and after their imprisonment. For example, Norma Peralta, whose story I shared earlier, said that her most vivid memory was of a compañera, Mónica Sotti, who later became her cellmate: "I remember when they were beating her, she started singing a *cuarteto* at the top of her lungs. This always stayed with me. I still remember the lyrics: 'This death is not on me; the one who loads is the one who kills.' She would be singing, and they would be beating her, but savagely" (Peralta, October 2008). The people of Córdoba are known for their appreciation for cuarteto, a type of folk music that originated in Córdoba and is rooted in the music of Italian and Spanish dance ensembles. Traditionally, cuarteto is played by a four-piece band (violin, piano, accordion, and bass), which gives the music its name. The music is fast-paced and upbeat, and it remains associated with the working class of Córdoba Province today. The image of Mónica singing a cuarteto is particularly powerful because many of the ex-presos were disappeared for seeking to improve the living conditions of the working class, and because a compañera was able to engage in something joyful while being beaten by her torturers. Norma said that although Mónica today suffers from serious long-term consequences of the meningitis that she contracted in prison, the image she still has of Mónica is of her refusing to give away any information to her torturers and singing so loudly that other compañeros could hear and remain steadfast through her act of defiance.

The rest of this chapter is about how the ex-presos themselves engaged in acts of solidarity and resistance, as recounted in their oral history archive interviews. Ex-presos expressed their stories of resistance in the various ways in which they continued to stand against oppression even as the military increasingly restricted their freedom in prison. Solidarity, a word that has particular significance in Latin American leftist groups for its expression of commitment to a political project, is an active form of "being there" for one's compañeros. Ex-presos would compliment others by describing them as *muy solidario*, or very much committed to the political project. The ex-presos repeatedly emphasized these two values, solidarity and resistance, in tours, at meetings, in writings, and during public presentations. The definitions employed here are based on my interpretation of how ex-presos defined the two values through their use of the words and through the types of stories they told to illustrate them. In seeking to share these stories of how prisoners resisted and expressed solidarity during their detention, I discuss four loosely gathered themes: community building, noncollaboration, education, and mental health care.

Community Building

Even though the military sought to separate prisoners and to turn them against one another through a combination of physical and psychological torture, the prisoners continued to find innovative ways to communicate with one another and to create a sense of regularity, control, and organization among themselves. Several ex-presos lectured me on the theory that one of the goals of the dictatorship's state terrorism was to create a culture of individualism: neighbors turned away when someone was abducted, the military using torture to break individuals and to stop them from protecting their compañeros. The ex-presos say that they resisted attempts by the military to undercut their collective identity by building a sense of community in prison. This community was, for many compañeros, also the ultimate sign of solidarity because without one another, survival would have been next to impossible.

AEPPC member Viviana "Vivi" Vergara remembered how her fellow women-prisoners helped her recover from torture and adjust to prison life. After suffering through numerous interrogation sessions at the concentration camp La Perla over the course of a month, and over five additional days at another concentration camp, La Ribera, Vivi was transferred to UP1, a regular prison. When a new prisoner would arrive, any resources that other prisoners had in possession were passed through the cells to the newcomer in hopes of giving some form of moral support. Vivi recalled her first day in UP1:

> When I got to UP1 I learned that the compañeras were using very crude tweezers for their eyebrows. Having spent so much time in the torture camps, we hadn't been able to tweeze and our eyebrows grew very thick! [laughing] They all knew that I was someone who had suffered like them. When I got to prison I was still bruised all over. When the girls passed along the tweezers to me so I could pluck—this was very kind of them—they also handed me the top of a milk can to use as a mirror, and when I peered into it, I could see that I was all black and purple and dark all over. When I looked in the mirror I said, "*Milicos* [derogatory slang for a military officer] sons of bitches! They gave me my first wrinkle!" [laughing] Out of all of the things that they had done to my body, I was still

vain. This just set them all off laughing, because it was a totally unexpected reaction. (Vergara, August 2008)

Vivi explained that when a new prisoner arrived, she would receive soap, a mirror, tweezers, and anything else the fellow prisoners had collected or created, because being tortured and sent to prison for the first time was the moment in which prisoners were the most vulnerable. Then, as soon as the next prisoner arrived, all of those resources would be passed along to her, and so on. After receiving help from others, Vivi wanted to return the favor by working to increase the morale of other prisoners. Because they were living in tiny cells that measured two by two meters (approximately 6.5 feet), with beds made of cement and constant fluorescent light, prisoners had to find ways to overcome the individual isolation in such a cramped and dank space:

> Some compañeros were very strong, very solid. I considered myself a strong compañera, particularly in comparison to others who were really depressed and didn't speak to anyone. Those who refused to be amused closed in on themselves. There was a group of us who were more resilient who would always try to speak with them, to help them. But there were serious issues; there were compañeras whose children had been taken from them and they didn't know where their children were. Others were dealing with their husbands having just been killed. Some of them just didn't want anything to do with anyone and remained distrustful. Still, we made every attempt to express our solidarity by finding moments of happiness—taking every opportunity to laugh about something, to imitate someone, to throw parties, and to perform a little theater. (Ibid)

Another way in which political prisoners built their community was by sharing any resources they obtained from the outside. Prisoners whose families knew where they were imprisoned, could sometimes receive packages, though no one package could provide enough of anything. The military inspected every package and, unsurprisingly, not all of the contents reached the intended recipient. In addition, not all families had the same financial means to send packages. As a result, the women-prisoners—there were about 120 of them—would share the contents of their packages, paying particular attention to those who were in acute need. "We shared everything, absolutely everything," said Vivi, "Whoever had the most would share with whoever needed something the most. If you had a gall bladder problem, they would give you aspirin" (Ibid.).

Another way in which women supported one another was through the "hair salon" created in Villa Devoto. Villa Devoto was one of the few prisons that did not place prisoners in isolation, allowed prisoners to receive packages, and permitted written communication between prisoners and family members. (During the dictatorship, Villa Devoto was usually the last prison women were transferred to before their release, if they had survived up to that point, and was used as a "showcase" by the military during visits by international human rights inspectors.) AEPPC member Élida "Ely" Eichenberger said the hair salon was particularly helpful for prisoners separated from their children:

> When letters would arrive for the compañeras from their children, it was really hard on them. It was then that the salon came to be. We made hair rollers out of old newspapers and we prepared the chemicals. We cooked sugar to make a liquid and used strips of cloth from old bed sheets to wax our legs. We did facials with creams for pimples or dry skin. We had requested creams from dermatologists for medical reasons but they were intended for the salon all along. Amid the craziness in a cell that was built to hold only about two prisoners, one would arrive to get waxed while siting on top of the bunk, another person below the bunk would be giving another a massage, and another would be in the corner reading a letter. It was a space of resistance: to share letters from their children with other compañeras, to share the experience of being mothers, and to share letters while we cared for ourselves as women. (Eichenberger, October 2008)

Ely explained that the women created an everyday space where, like in a real salon, women would talk about their families while receiving beauty treatments. It was a space of resistance because, as Ely said, "We were finding ways to survive, to find moments of happiness and self-care at the same time as the military was trying to destroy us" (Ibid.).

Sometimes the acts of solidarity were more confrontational. Vivi recounted the time she and fellow prisoners staged a protest to keep their cell doors open longer and demanded to speak with Third Army Corps General Menéndez: "One day we planted ourselves at the bottom of the doors to our cells and refused to go inside. We sat in front so that the prison guards couldn't close the doors. Some of the other compañeras said, 'You are all crazy.' [laughing] 'Why would you want Menéndez to come here?' They were right about us because some terrible things had already happened to some of the prisoners there. They had already taken out some compañeros, men and women, who were then executed" (Vergara, August 2008). For the women-prisoners who knew about the killings that took place at UP1, the idea of protesting and asking to see Menéndez was indeed "crazy." These women were demanding to speak with the general who had ordered all of the disappearances and killings in Córdoba Province, and who presumably had no sympathy for those he considered to be subversive. In the end, Vivi said, a police chief came in place of Menéndez and promised to relay their message. He told them to enter their cells for the time being and that he would pass along the request and not punish them. At four in the morning, military officers took out six compañeras from their cells, Vivi among them. They were taken to the patio, where they were tortured with a mock execution in punishment for their protest. Afterward, these six compañeras were placed in complete isolation.

Prisoners broke the rules together, because it was a way of building community, especially if it meant that they could find a way to pass the time and entertain one another. Ely, with her theater background, directed shows during prisoners' weekly showers in UP1, even though they were prohibited from speaking to one another: "I was taken to the punishment cell for doing theater inside. [laughter] We put on shows on Saturdays in the shower stalls. The shower room was more or less pretty spacious. The showers were separated by short walls, and in the more open space was where we left our towels and where the audience sat. Then in this space [using her fingers to draw on the table], where you exited from the showers, is where we performed the plays. There were like eighty people in our cellblock. So we did four performances: twenty, twenty, twenty, twenty. . . . It was important to introduce the compañeras to theater and to do it themselves" (Eichenberger, October 2008).

Ely explained in her interview that a particular compañera wanted to perform, so Ely staged the performances to fulfill her wish. The fact that Ely directed four different shows also demonstrates the degree to which the prisoners organized themselves. Although prisoners were punished with isolation when they were caught breaking the rules, Ely continued to direct the theatrical performances because the sense of community sustained her and her fellow prisoners.

The men also created a sense of community in prison. Juan Carlos Álvarez remembered that on December 13, 1976, while in a prison in Resistencia, a city in the northern province of Chaco, he and his cellmates attempted to stop the military from taking away thirteen prisoners in the middle of the night. They knew that the prisoners who were taken out in this manner were most likely going to be executed: "We pressed ourselves against the prison bars and reached out to try to stop them from being about to leave. We were trying to negotiate, and the guard who had entered the cell block said, 'It's better that they leave now because the army is coming in to take over, and it'll be worse if they take them out'" (Álvarez, February 2009). At the time that this happened, the military had not yet taken over this particular prison even though the coup had already taken place on March 24, 1976. Still, the prisoners knew that the conditions were worsening, particularly since more captives were killed at the beginning of the dictatorship than at any other point. Many of the prisoners, such as Juan Carlos, had been imprisoned before the coup, and were now witnessing the rapidly deteriorating conditions. For this reason, he and others were frantically trying to stop the guards from "transferring" prisoners:

> And we started to try to communicate with other prisoners by shouting out to them, trying to find a way out of this, to figure out a way to negotiate with the guards to stop them from taking prisoners. And then we had to let one of the prisoners go from the first prison block. We had no way of stopping other ones from leaving. In order to communicate with each other, we had to use the little windows— every cell had a little window that we used to communicate with one another. Normally we communicated with one another using our hands, but in this situation we were screaming. It was a desperate situation and we were expecting the worst. From our prison block they took away four compañeros, and I think the total number of prisoners taken was thirteen. (Ibid.)

That night, these prisoners who were taken out of their cells, along with other prisoners from a different prison, were tortured and then executed. The bodies of twenty-two prisoners were disposed in unmarked graves, and these killings became known as the Massacre of Margarita Belén.

Non-Collaboration

From the beginning, guerrillas and committed leftist activists knew that they ran the risk of being kidnapped and imprisoned as in previous dictatorship eras, but they did not know about—or were not prepared for—the torture they would undergo. However, as more and more of those around them disappeared, and as survivors came out with testimonies of what had happened to them, compañeros became more aware. They learned that they had to develop strategies to withstand torture and not to give up names, locations, or organizational information. By not giving up information to the military, the compañeros were both resisting torture and showing solidarity by sacrificing themselves rather than not naming others. Despite accusations that survival was connected to giving others away, the AEPPC members said that they were able to resist giving up information to the military precisely because they were politically prepared prior to their fall.

The ex-presos interviewed in this research were part of political organizations, and through these organizations, they were trained, or rather instructed, not to speak under torture. For example, AEPPC member Ester Cabral, who was a member of the PRT, was specifically trained to resist giving up any names or addresses for at least four days after being kidnapped, in order to give her compañeros time to escape the military. Before she was abducted, Ester had a premonition to relocate. Her former partner, Juan José, nicknamed "Negro,"[8] had arrived in Misiones, where she was living with a Paraguayan family. Ester was about to flee with him and another compañera, but while she was packing, she changed her mind and decided to stay. She was tired of being on the run; she had a newborn baby, Nora. Shortly thereafter, the military found Ester and disappeared her to a torture camp.

Ironically, Ester had gone through a similar situation with Negro, in Córdoba. A compañero told Ester that the military was coming for Negro because someone had named him under torture and revealed the address of the factory where he worked. Ester went to the factory and told the manager that she needed to see Negro; his father had died, she said. Negro came out of the factory crying, and Ester had to explain that what she had said earlier was a lie and that they needed to escape immediately. They got into a taxi and left Córdoba, which is how they ended up in Misiones, where the tables were essentially turned. (Later, Negro would tell Ester that he wished he had given her an incentive to leave, so that she would not have fallen into the hands of the military.) When Ester was kidnapped, the military took Nora as well, and the baby was with her when she was interrogated and tortured for one specific purpose: the military wanted to know Negro's whereabouts. Ester remembered hearing Nora screaming while she was blindfolded and being tortured; the military told her that they were torturing her baby: "Maybe because I'm skinny with small bones—I was able to slip out of my handcuffs. I was constantly trying to readjust them. I took off my blindfold and I saw a guy in the corner trying to prop her up. They weren't torturing her but it was bad that she had been watching me be tortured" (Cabral, November 2008). After catching a glimpse of Nora, Ester did not hear or see her daughter again, except when her torturers taunted her by saying that Nora was "now being raised by others," and that she was "no longer going to be a subversive" (Ibid.). Knowing already that children had been stolen from other women-prisoners, Ester felt anguish when her torturers informed her that Nora had been given up to a military family, and for the next four days, she was systematically beaten and told that she was going to be killed. "Come what may, we had instructions to withstand the torture," said Ester (Ibid.), and she did not talk for four days. Then she admitted that she was part of the PRT and gave the name of someone she knew was already dead, a tactic the PRT had adopted in anticipation of interrogation sessions. Ester remembered that a woman named Clara had just died and used her name. Ester and her compañeros memorized names of subversives from year-old newspaper reports of alleged shoot-outs so that they could be used to buy time for other compañeros. "You also tried not to say where you actually came from, so if you were from Córdoba, you would say that you were from Buenos Aires; that way they couldn't get information from someone from the same province," said Ester.

On the fifth day, the torturers left Ester with a doctor because she had developed mastitis, as she was still breastfeeding Nora at the time. "I was all swollen, bruised, and in horrific pain," said Ester (Ibid.). Though they were torturing Ester and threatening to kill her, the military allowed the doctor to give Ester antibiotics for her mastitis and time to stop her milk supply. It was during this time that Ester started considering whether she should collaborate to get back her daughter. "The story was that if you collaborated, you could get back your child. I had heard this from other guerrillas when their kids were given away to others. I told myself that if I didn't collaborate, they were going to keep me in a concentration camp and that it wasn't going to be easy," said Ester (Ibid.).

Still, Ester said that she chose not to collaborate. Instead she was loaded onto a truck with other captives, who she said looked "utterly physically and psychologically destroyed" (Ibid.). She was taken to a concentration camp in Misiones, where she was tortured over and over again. She was then transferred to another concentration camp where she was "tortured under a bright light, while the radio played loudly and groups of men continually humiliated me" (Ibid.). Afterward, Ester was transferred to a prison in Chaco, where the military brought in people who could potentially identify her. Fortunately, however, Ester had not gone out much before her abduction because she had been first pregnant, and was later at home with her first baby, in an unfamiliar town. Because she did not have a lot of social contact with others, there were few people who could recognize her by name. In a further attempt to break Ester, the military brought in a crying baby while she was hooded and told her that the baby was Nora and that she could hold her again if only she told them where Negro was located. Negro was highly sought after because he was one of the leaders in his political organization. But Ester knew it wasn't her baby's cry and refused to give up any information about Negro. Consequently, Ester was taken to another concentration camp to be tortured again. This time they poured water on her and then applied electric shocks all over her body. Without having any information for the military, Ester eventually got transferred to a regular prison, where she was able to communicate with other political prisoners.

Once in prison, Ester learned that her daughter, Nora, was being cared for by some regular prisoners. Using the channels of communication that the political prisoners developed with the regular prisoners, Ester was able to verify that Nora was in the same prison by describing specific birthmarks and the baby bag that Ester had carried around for Nora. The regular prisoners continued to take care of Nora until, with help from their local church, Ester's parents were able to claim Nora from prison. Ester remained in prison for five years and was released in 1982, under supervised release.

If "to sing" meant to give up information, *abrir los cantos* (lit. "to open up songs") meant to give up messages that prisoners had hidden on their bodies during inspections. Ex-preso Pedro Nolasco Gaetán believed that prisoners' political backgrounds influenced whether someone opened up the songbook, or revealed a hidden message in a bodily orifice. Pedro believed that those who suffered the most after they were freed, were those who broke under torture or who were unwilling to resist the military in prison, those who came from the left but hadn't been authentically committed to the broader political project, and those who were part of the wrong political party. He said it all depended upon on a compañero's "personal background, the type of organization or political preparation one had, and the level of comprehension he or she had about the political situation in Argentina and the reason for the revolutionary movements" (Gaetán, November 2008). For example, Pedro, who was a Peronist, believed that the Montoneros sang less often than members of the Argentine Communist Party:

> We carried messages in little bits of plastic, wrapping bits of cellophane around the pieces of paper to make a suppository, which we then put up our asses. Then after we had gone out and returned, we would take them out, wash them, and then read whatever news others had. Sometimes the guards would find out about this, and they would order us to open up. We didn't want to spread our legs, but the guys who were from the Communist Party and other vague leftist types did whatever they were told to do. They didn't even try to resist at all! The ability to resist, I still believe, had everything to do with your political and social background. Some compañeros had been broken, but very few of them—I can count them all on one hand. (Ibid.)

Pedro is critical of those prisoners who did not put up a fight to protest the guards and to protect the messages that they were ferrying around for others, but is at the same time careful to say that few prisoners broke under the pressure. Still, what is significant is that Pedro believes that there is a relationship between one's ability to resist giving up information, and one's political preparation prior to being kidnapped. For the ex-presos who tell stories of resistance, refusing to submit to bodily inspections, like in the Battle of the Panties, was illustrative of their political commitments in prison.

Education

Certain knowledge was considered subversive under the dictatorship. In particular, intellectuals were targeted by the dictatorship for both believing in dangerous, subversive ideas and disseminating them. It was ironic, then, that political prisoners learned more in prison than they had prior to their abduction. Educating one another in prison was a form of resistance. Not only were prisoners continuing to engage in ideas considered dangerous, but it was also a form of solidarity: they helped one another maintain their mental and physical health when they had nothing but their specialized knowledge in their empty cells. Sara Liliana Waitman used her skills as a physical education teacher to instruct her fellow prisoners on simple exercises to perform in their tiny cells to keep their muscles working. Viviana "Vivi" Vergara listened intently to the imprisoned professors who spoke about their particular fields: history, literature, and the arts. Vivi spoke about the "classes" she took in prison:

> We waited for people to give their classes in the mornings. There was a writer. There was a film student who had seen every film. There was another compañera who was a professor of linguistics. Another one was an accountant. That's how we spent our time: we would lie under our blankets while one person gave a class as soon as the guards were standing far away from us. The person's voice would pass through the hallway because our individual cells were lined up next to one another in a row. There were twenty cells on one side and another twenty on the other. The one person spoke

in a loud voice and everyone else listened. There was once a lecture about books that I had never read before, and that I only know about through what these compañeras told me, books by Jorge Luis Borges, Roberto Arlt, Joseph Maréchal. And I also learned about movies that I have still never seen just by what the compañera had recounted to me. Everything was done orally because we had absolutely nothing, except combs. (Vergara, August, 2008)

Tzvetan Todorov, in *Facing the Extreme: Moral Life in the Concentration Camps*, argues that attending to the "life of the mind" in extreme situations, like in concentration camps during the Holocaust, is a form of moral action (Todorov 1996 [1991], 92–96). The ex- presos performed "ordinary virtues" in order to maintain their sense of humanity (Ibid.,107). The ex-presos who had little formal education were delighted to have learned from the imprisoned intellectuals, and became, in the end, more educated on the subversive ideas that the military attempted to keep from the public.

Holding classes in prison also required solidarity on the part of the prisoners because everyone had to agree not to make noise during the classes. Only that way could everyone hear the person speaking, across all of the cells and down into the hallway. It also required that one of the prisoners should be on the lookout for incoming guards and to develop a code to warn others. There were two primary ways in which prisoners communicated. When giving classes or passing on information, prisoners communicated with one another through small keyholes from their individual cells. This activity required solidarity because it required communal silence to allow the voices to travel through the holes one at a time. Another form of communication was through Morse code. AEPPC member Gladys Regalado felt particularly grateful to the regular prisoners for teaching them Morse code because, without the ability to secretly communicate, they would have not been able to pass information along to the male political prisoners, who were held on a different floor than the women: "I remember when they brought a group of compañeros from Río Cuarto Province and they put them in the cells below ours, in the same pavilion but below us. I made friends with a compañero, speaking in Morse, and we passed the entire night speaking to each other using Morse code. We would have to check every so often to make sure that the guards weren't doing their rounds or else we would have been punished" (Regalado, September 2008).

AEPPC member Fidel Antonio Alcázar argued that he learned more about politics in prison than he did before—in fact, he became politicized after spending time with his compañeros and listening to them from his cell:

> I changed after I got out of prison. I had acquired a profound amount of knowledge in prison, on politics and history. I learned about things that I didn't even know were important to know: about wars, the French Revolution, what "ideology" meant, Marx, and a new perspective on the church. I learned the entire history of the Catholic Church from inside prison. I immersed myself into the humanities, so that I now had an internal life and not just an exterior life of manual labor, something I still do today. My previous life wasn't entirely erased, because I still work in maintenance today, even though I am no longer the same person with the same goals that I once had. Things like technology, advances in science, were topics that changed me completely because then I started to look at my old life differently. It was like I dedicated myself more to things; I began to participate in politics, and go to political meetings, and I had a lot of contact with people in politics. I hadn't done these things before and I began to be more engaged politically. (Alcázar, October 2008)

Because not all of those who were kidnapped had the same level of political commitment, knowledge, or even background, there was a lot of potential for prisoners to learn from one another. As mentioned more than once before, the prisoners would share their knowledge with one another as a way to pass time, to keep their minds active, and to resist the conditions in which they were placed. Antonio learned that he knew little about the world, and being shut up in a prison with those who knew a lot about history, politics, and religion ended up exposing him to more knowledge than before. The greatest irony is that while the military attempted to depoliticize militants by punishing and torturing them, Antonio explained that he became politicized precisely because of what he learned in prison.

In her interview, María del Carmen "Carmencita" Pérez, who was imprisoned in 1978, for her activities as a Montonera and released in 1983, remarked that homemakers who were imprisoned because of their husbands' labor or political activities and had no political background, also became political from being around other militants. "In general, prisoners were all youths, but there were quite a few older compañeras. There were a lot of homemakers; the wives were imprisoned mostly because of their husbands rather than for their [own] ideologies. A lot of the wives of political prisoners were kidnapped with their husbands, and then they learned about politics in prison. Before prison they knew nothing, and later they left as serious activists" (Pérez, August 2008). The military tried to imprison anyone who even thought in a way that ran counter to its own ideologies, and yet these intellectuals were able to share their ideas through the prison walls. These are the types of stories that the ex-presos share with youths during tours at D2. They also direct attention to the fact that the dictatorship viewed thought, intellectualism, education, and certain fields of study as subversive. In turn, the students only then realize that in an earlier era, they would have been at risk, as they shared the same interest in sociology or music as those who were imprisoned for being subversive.

Mental Health Care

Holocaust survivor Viktor E. Frankl, who believed that cultivating meaning in one's life was crucial in surviving the concentration camps, wrote, in *Man's Search for Meaning*, "The prisoner who lost faith in the future—his future—was doomed. With his loss of belief in the future, he also lost his spiritual gold; he let himself decline and became subject to mental and physical decay" (Frankl 1985 [1946], 95). Staying mentally sane or healthy was a major concern for prisoners who were regularly subjected to psychological forms of torture. Élida "Ely" Eichenberger recalled being punished and sent to the isolation cell, but she also recalled the strategies she adopted to keep her sanity. First, Ely described how she ended up in the *celda de castigo* (punishment cell) three times: "When I was in prison I was very concerned about my mental health. Before I was released from prison, I spent almost three months straight in the punishment cell. They would let me go out in the morning but I would have to return in the afternoon. [laughter] My take on it, or my analysis of the situation, was that they already knew that I was going to be fine to be let out under supervised release, so they put me through a process to make me come out very delicate while being under supervised release, to make me feel vulnerable"(Eichenberger, October 2008). In hindsight, Ely believed that, because the military knew they were going to release her from prison, they wanted to subject her to psychological and physical torture in the punishment cell so that she would be brought down to her knees when she had her freedom. Initially, Ely was sent to the punishment cell because she had participated in the Battle of the Panties, refusing to submit to a bodily inspection. She was given fifteen days in the punishment cell and, on the last day, while she was bathing, the guard told her to hurry up and finish. In reaction, Ely covered herself up and told the guard to leave. "I was angry about having to bathe in front of this crazy lady," said Ely. "Well, then I got a month" (Ibid.). On the day that she was let out of the punishment cell, as she was walking down to return to the political prisoners' regular cells, she came across a guard carrying the mail. The guard accused Ely of giving her a bad look, and so she was sent back upstairs to the punishment cell. After her punishment was carried out, she was let out again and, right before she joined the other political prisoners outside in the patio, she heard the guard say "Eichenberger. Stay in your cell." When Ely asked why, she was told, "Because you were talking." Ely then protested, "I wasn't talking." The guard said, "Yes, you are; you're speaking right now" (Ibid.). Ely was immediately sent back to the punishment cell.

In order to cope with her time in the punishment cell, Ely found ways to keep her mind occupied to preserve her mental sanity: "On the fourth day, you start to ask yourself, 'Why me?' And when you've reached that point in asking the 'why me?' question, it's downhill—you go to shit. You're totally fucked. So the challenge was to organize your little head so you don't end up in that boat. Because when you start to entertain that question, that's when you fall into a depression. . . . In the punishment cell, there is no compañera who will say to you, 'Here, take my hand!' There is no compañera who is going to encourage you and say, 'Come on, you have to be brave. You have to be strong!'" (Ibid.). What made the punishment cell challenging and different from being in other cells was that you were shut out completely, and there was no one else near the cell. Below, in the regular cells, even if the prisoners could not see one another, they could at least hear one another. They could extend a hand, metaphorically, to another prisoner who was struggling. A sense of community was important in helping one another survive prison.

To better understand the kind of mental work that Ely engaged in while she was in the punishment cell, I asked her what specifically she meant by "organizing your little head."

> During those three months that I was in the [punishment] cell, I had organized everything like this: in the morning, when I woke up—they woke me up at six-thirty [she taps her finger on the table], and then they took the mattress away from me. They didn't leave you with it; they took it out. I would then take advantage when the *bicha* (snake), the *pistola* (gun), [referring to the prison guard] was busy doing other things. I would do exercises. Then the *mate cocido* [herbal tea] would come. I would drink the mate cocido. Then I would do mental exercises in math. For example, looking at the surface of the wall, of the window, I would do mental calculations of the measurements. The surface of the concrete bed—the bed had all of these holes [in the bedspring], so then, while I focused on one of the holes, I would figure out how many, how much space was metal, and how much was space in between the holes, in my head. I did all of those mental calculations to work the mind, to work on logic. (Ibid.)

Through these activities, Ely prevented herself from falling into the existential crisis of "why me?"

One common theme that emerged from the interviews was the importance of keeping up one's hygiene and appearance, which provided many with a sense of dignity or something intangible, mental or emotional, that helped them live through the indignities of concentration camps. Gladys Regalado was known for her preening, immaculate appearance, and femininity, and shared how she maintained her tweezing and waxing:

> In the prison here in Córdoba [UP1], I was always doing myself up, being very coquettish. All of the girls made fun of me because I was worried about my hair. I straightened my hair but without rollers, without anything, because we didn't have anything. I tweezed while looking into the top of the Nido milk can. The girls always teased me and said, ". . . even though she's in prison, she tweezes

and straightens her hair." Well, those kinds of things were what the girls remembered about prison because when one is all locked up in there, who cares if you're pretty or ugly when no one is going to see you? But, well, it made me feel good. (Regalado, September 2008)

The energy Gladys put into caring for herself even when she had very little with which to improve her appearance, kept her mentally strong. Taking care of herself was her form of resistance to the prison conditions she was subjected to and to the denial of comforts that would enable prisoners to have an individual identity. Tweezing and straightening her hair gave Gladys control over her appearance, and therefore, her identity.

Recognition for Solidarity and Resistance

For Juan Carlos Álvarez the most meaningful experience he had after his release from prison was when the Spanish ambassador met with him and with other political prisoners without advance notice. They had gone to see him and to discuss why, after they were granted visas from Spain, the Argentine government prohibited them from leaving the country: "We went to see the ambassador and he said to us, 'We lived through Franco; I understand the struggle that you are going through.' There were about three or four of us. He said, 'Thank you for having come to visit me. It a chance for us to tell you—we also in fact have political exiles in several countries for having suffered a terrible dictatorship under Franquismo— that you should stand tall and proud and remain citizens'" (Álvarez, February 2009). Juan Carlos said the ambassador gave them advice, and that he began to cry when the ambassador shook his hand and embraced him while saying that he hoped that his children would become like Argentine youths one day—that they would know what it means to fight for a democracy. The ambassador at one point, said Juan Carlos, even offered them money, which they refused, and told them that the doors to the Spanish embassy would always be open to them. When I asked Juan Carlos why this encounter had been so meaningful, he said, "It was important because he was the first person, apart from the human rights organizations that fought for us, to treat us well. To have appreciation for our activism" (Ibid.). Juan Carlos wanted others to have respect for the fact that he endured imprisonment for a righteous cause. Rather than being blamed for his imprisonment and accused of being a terrorist or having committed an act of betrayal, he wanted to be seen in a positive light. When the Spanish ambassador said that Juan Carlos was a role model for his children, it gave him a sense of validation. By telling stories of how they expressed solidarity and continued to resist the military from inside prison, the ex-presos establish themselves as committed activists and as morally upright citizens. Thus, more important than the fact that they were tortured is why they were tortured in the first place. Passing on memories of solidarity and resistance remind others of the fact that they are not just torture victims, but political and moral agents.

For the better part of the three decades since the dictatorship ended, ex-presos were regarded as terrorists, traitors, or torture victims. Élida "Ely" Eichenberger was quoted earlier saying, "former political prisoners have to position [themselves] in a different place in history." Their stories of resistance and solidarity attest to the fact that they were tortured and imprisoned for the political threat they posed to the dictatorship. Similarly, in an exchange between ESMA survivor Munú Actis and ex-presa Mirta Clara, the question of survivor guilt is best answered by remembering that they were imprisoned for political reasons:

MUNÚ: Mirta, I don't know whether this happens to you all. We feel the guilt of being alive, although during the course of our meetings, the guilt started to shrink.

MIRTA: That guilt is in everyone; it's in those who left, in those who stayed, in those of us who experienced imprisonment. I always say that some day we'll have to honor ourselves for what we are, for what we fought for and still fight for. (Actis et al. 2006, 296)

The AEPPC members are finding ways to honor themselves and their fallen compañeros through their stories of resistance and solidarity in prison, when they still held onto their ideals despite the military's attempt to break them. They want recognition not simply for having suffered torture, but for being part of a larger political struggle that was worth fighting for. Kelly McKinney, in "Breaking the Conspiracy of Silence: Testimony, Traumatic Memory, and Psychotherapy with Survivors of Political Violence," wrote, "[C]linicians may subordinate social needs of clients to the ethical call to bear witness, neglect to acknowledge the nuanced moral complexity of political violence, and lose sight of the understanding that traumatic memories are politically and culturally mediated. As a result, an ideology may crystallize that casts clients as innocent victims, paradoxically denying a sense of their full moral and psychological agency rather than restoring it" (McKinney 2007, 266–267)

5

Life After Prison
Still Feels Like Imprisonment

"I could deal with being physically tortured, but what I couldn't deal with was having been separated from my daughter [Ceci] and my husband," said AEPPC member Alicia Staps. "It was very painful for me to not have been able to see Ceci during all of those years. To see her after she had gotten so big, walking and talking. She no longer recognized me" (Staps, November 2008). When asked about the lasting consequences of their imprisonment for their lives afterward, ex-presos' answers were similar to Alicia's in that they spent little time directly discussing the trauma they suffered from torture. Instead, they spoke at length about their broken relationships and about their disappointment that their lives turned out differently than they had imagined.

As discussed in chapter 4, ex-presos avoided speaking about their torture experiences even if they suffered from the aftereffects. Speaking about torture would have undermined their identities as activists and reinforced their images as helpless victims. However, it is also the case, as I will argue in this chapter, that ex-presos held a broader understanding of what constituted a violation. Violations were not limited to what happened in prison, but also included the secondary effects that impacted them over the course of their lives. For this reason, prisoners did not necessarily feel liberated once they were released from prison.

Ex-presos repeatedly said that they suffered from *secuelas de terrorismo del estado* (effects of state terrorism). The labor activist, Juan Villa, who also worked to oversee the provincial census of political prisoners for the

Secretariat of Human Rights of Córdoba, explained that state terrorism "was the whole apparatus that the military imposed upon society to bring citizens down to their knees" (personal conversation, May 2009). In the case of those who were activists, the military state used more directed forms of terror that included not only disappearances, torture, and illegal imprisonment, but also monitoring and job dismissals. "These methods of state repression were used to implement political and economic policies against the interests of the *pueblo* [lit. translated "the people," but this term refers to the working class or the masses]," said Juan (Ibid.). Thus, ex-presos view many mundane parts of their lives, such as gaining employment, as touched by the dictatorship's methods of state terrorism. In other words, it wasn't simply that they were tortured and had to live in degrading conditions in prison. Being subjected to torture and imprisonment meant that rather than realizing their political dreams, they came out of prison having to rebuild their families, to reintegrate themselves into hostile and fearful communities, and to face the stigma of having once been a political prisoner when seeking work.

That victims of state violence regard the socioeconomic impacts of their imprisonment as a steep price for their activism is unsurprising, as other scholars have also written on this topic (David and Yuk-ping 2005; Robins 2011). What is surprising, however, is the demand for repeated compensation for the enduring impacts of imprisonment. As discussed in chapter 4, ex-presos mentioned torture in public appearances as a reason for their struggle to win more reparations, but what they have found troubling as they age, are the challenges they faced after their release from prison, which continued to impact them over the duration of their lives. The AEPPC, along with other groups of ex-presos, want reparation for suffering they experienced on a social and economic level because they see their ongoing struggles as linked to what the military had done to them three decades ago.

Several scholars have criticized past transitional justice processes for limiting their mandates to a narrow set of human rights abuses, particularly civil and political violations, and for failing to alleviate entrenched socioeconomic inequalities under new political regimes (Laplante 2008; Miller 2008; Muvingi 2009). These same scholars are focused on the macrolevel, examining the roots of inequality that led to the conflict, and that continue to endure or have the potential to create new conflict. My research also reveals the limitations of Argentina's transitional justice process in

addressing the socioeconomic impacts of stigma attached to imprisonment. However, I am not speaking about the general political critique of
the economic policies advocated and practiced by the military and by the
political elites, which ex-presos and other leftists believe have widened
the socioeconomic gap between the rich and the poor. I am speaking instead
about how ex-presos were personally impacted by their imprisonment.

In discussing how ex-presos spoke about the long-term impacts of
imprisonment, I draw upon Veena Das's description of how the past affects
the present in her book, *Life and Words: Violence and the Descent into the Ordinary*. Das demonstrates how the violence surrounding the Partition of India
in 1947, and the assassination of then prime minister, Indira Gandhi, in
1984, seeps into the lives of individuals and the collective in ordinary ways—
long after the events. The violence of the past comes to structure the everyday. Das describes her intent to write about violence by saying that her book
"narrates the lives of particular persons and communities who were deeply
embedded in these events, and it describes the way that the event attaches
itself with its tentacles into everyday life and folds itself into the recesses
of the ordinary" (Das 2006, 1). In other words, the rupture and the violence
that erupts become incorporated into the lives of individuals over time.

The suffering that the ex-presos spoke about in their interviews was
not constrained to the time that they were imprisoned and tortured. Their
imprisonment was the rupture, the event. But they spoke about the time
after their release—how their ordinary lives are connected to past violent
events. For the ex-presos, perhaps paradoxically, it was during life after
incarceration that they most felt the impact of what had happened to
them. These long-term effects that the ex-presos suffered—social, political, and economic—affected the way in which they are aging and left them
mourning for what could have been, had they not been imprisoned. Long-
term impacts of imprisonment fell under four common themes: internal
exile, broken partnerships, job discrimination, and family strain.

Internal Exile

Many ex-presos were displaced within Argentina to avoid being kidnapped
during the dictatorship, and they lived in *exilio interno* (internal exile).
Even without leaving the country, those in internal exile found themselves

feeling lonely and isolated. To prevent their family members from being put in a situation in which they might give away their hideout under interrogation, ex-presos never disclosed their locations. Constantly moving around made it difficult or impossible to hold a steady job, to create a stable environment for children, and to maintain relationships with friends and family who could otherwise provide social support.

In the end, living in exile internally meant a complete loss of identity, because ex-presos had to drop all political activities, shed themselves of their real names, and pretend to be someone else. ESMA survivor Munú Actis explained why internal exile continues to impact survivors even today:

> Internal exile was a terrible thing, and it still is to this day. If you were living abroad, even though you missed a lot of things, at some level there was a social acknowledgment. "Poor thing, you had to leave," they'd say. The people who stayed behind had to just swallow it all the time. Those of us in exile could talk—we needed to talk to survive; those who stayed in the country had to keep quiet to survive. Among the people who stayed, there were those who disappeared from the place where they lived, left their families and friends, and reappeared somewhere else with a trumped-up story to explain how they'd turned up there. And today they are not acknowledged. (Actis et al. 2006, 76)

Munú describes precisely why ex-presos cited internal exile as an injury—they were silenced and uprooted from everything they had known, and their suffering was never acknowledged publicly or considered a violation meriting reparation. Yet, internal exile was extremely common: twenty-three of the thirty-nine ex-presos interviewed were forced into internal exile.

A Young Couple, a Baby,
and a Little Citroën: A Story of Internal Exile

Alicia Staps was one of the ex-presos who lived for an extended time in internal exile. After majoring in social work at a university in Rosario, Alicia enrolled in a postgraduate program at the Christian Institute of Social Study and Political Action. Most of her professors were Peronists and part of the Third World movement, and they strongly shaped Alicia's political consciousness—even though she had previously held a negative view of Peronismo. (In 1953, when she was eight years old, her father had been fired for not joining the Peronist Party.) Alicia had worked in various social outreach programs that served the poor.

Through this work, Alicia met Manuel, a student of psychology and a Montonero. After they were married and had their first child, Cecilia ("Ceci"), Manuel fell, in 1970, under Juan Carlos Onganía's dictatorship, and was imprisoned at Enclausados. Compañeros warned Alicia that the military was coming after her, and that she needed to live underground or else face the risk of being tortured. Because Alicia needed to escape, she was forced to leave Ceci, who was only three months old at the time, in Rosario with her parents. "When I went into hiding, I didn't dare take her with me because I didn't know what was going to happen. If they killed me, what would happen to her? That's why I didn't want to take her. It was terrible, all that I suffered from having to leave her. I can't even explain it to you—how I cried about leaving my three-month-old baby behind" (Staps, November 2008). Though it was extremely painful to be separated from her daughter, Alicia feared even more the possibility of her child being kidnapped, tortured, or made to watch Alicia be tortured, all of which had already happened to other children.

Despite having moved to another province—Tucumán, in the northern part of the country—, Alicia fell in August 1971, and was imprisoned for two years. The military first kidnapped Alicia and held her incommunicado. Then they transferred her to Villa Devoto in Buenos Aires. Alicia remembered Villa Devoto as the place "where all of the fifty women- prisoners in the country were congregated" in the years between 1971 and 1973.

After spending eight months, from August to March, in Villa Devoto, Alicia was transferred to Rawson, the country's highest-security prison, located in the southern province of Chubut. At Rawson, two wards were created for women, and approximately one hundred women were transferred there from Villa Devoto. Following a prison break in August 1972, the women- prisoners were transferred back to Villa Devoto. Soon after, Alicia was transferred to Córdoba, where she was supposed to be put on trial, but it never materialized. Instead, she was taken to Buen Pastor, a regular prison for women that had been established by the Sisters of Our Lady of Clarity of the Good Pastor of Angers in 1906. However, the Catholic nuns who ran Buen Pastor refused Alicia entry because she had been caught with a compañero who was labeled *máxima peligrosidad* (extremely dangerous): "In Buen Pastor there had been several prison breaks. Well, there were at least three of them. So, when they saw the front cover of my file, they said that the guerrillas would attempt another break-in to rescue me. But I wasn't actually the dangerous one. Rather, it was my compañero who I fell with—I was considered extremely dangerous because of him. Even INTERPOL (International Police) was looking for him. But he wasn't dangerous either; he was an excellent compañero. But to the military, he was very dangerous because he was a Montonero leader" (Ibid.). Since Alicia was rejected from Buen Pastor, the military instead transferred her to a men's prison, Enclausados. However, the military did not place Alicia on the second floor with the male political prisoners. Instead, Alicia was sent to the ward reserved for rapists: "There were about fifty rapists. There was a little room that was inside the ward. There was only one room and tiny like this [she draws a small rectangle around her body with her index fingers] and it could only fit a mattress. When I entered, I stood in front of a filthy mattress full of bed bugs. I'll never forget how disgusting it was. . . . It was the room that they used to lock someone in when there was a problem with one of the rapists. It was the punishment cell" (Ibid.). Alicia was held in Enclausados from November 1972, until her release in May 1973. After the fall of Gen. Alejandro Lanusse's dictatorship, Alicia and her husband were both released under President Héctor José Cámpora's amnesty. President Cámpora, who was in office between May 25 and July 13, 1973, freed all of the political prisoners who had been detained during the dictatorial period known as the Argentine Revolution.

Under the new government, Alicia and Manuel continued their political activism, even as their imprisonment had come at a great cost to their daughter: "When we were freed we went to see Ceci and everyone told her, 'That's your mama and your daddy.' And she took one look at us and then hid behind her grandparents, because she didn't recognize us. She didn't want to have anything to do with us. We wanted to take her back. It was awful. She made a scene, cried, and kicked. So we left her with her grandparents. Then we adopted a strategy where we visited her every day. We went to see her, to be with her, to feed her, and to change her clothes, so that she could get to know her parents" (Ibid.). Alicia said it was overwhelming because not only was Ceci robbed of her parents at an early age, but they felt that they were taking her away from the only parents she knew—her grandparents—when they were released. After several months, Alicia and Manuel took their daughter home with them, despite her "crying and kicking in protest." A year after they were freed from prison, in 1974, Alicia and Manuel were forced into exile once again. Under Isabel Martínez's presidency (1974–1976), the *Alianza Anticomunista Argentina* (Argentine Anti-Communist Alliance, or Triple A) began killing left-wing Peronists. In Córdoba, various labor leaders had already been imprisoned, and when Alicia's compañeros informed her that she was being actively pursued again, she and Manuel moved to Mar del Plata. Manuel's uncle, a retired military officer, offered his nephew a job at a hotel. However, even those with family members in the military were not immune to disappearance. When the military began killing leftists in Mar del Plata, they fled to Uruguay in 1975.[1] Life became even more precarious when the military in Argentina staged a coup on March 24, 1976.

Like others who had gone underground, Alicia and Manuel moved far away from their hometowns to the most obscure towns they could find in the most remote rural areas. They concealed their pasts and assumed new identities until they had to move again. Their ability to escape on a moment's notice was only possible thanks to financial support from Alicia's parents.

After being tracked down in Uruguay, Alicia and Manuel escaped to a rural town in Argentina with Ceci, their second daughter, Mechi, and a third child on the way. (Moving to another Latin American country did not ensure anyone's safety since all of the countries in the Southern Cone were sharing intelligence under a military operation known as Project Condor.) Manuel explained to strangers that they had moved to the small town so that he could work as a beekeeper, and they moved next door to a police officer and his wife. Although the police worked with the military to disappear people, Alicia and Manuel had assumed new identities that included friendship with a police officer. While Alicia and Manuel held vastly different political views from their neighbors, the four of them held frequent weekend barbecues and spent time together through their children. They created an image of themselves as simply "a young couple with two little kids and their little Citroën."

Alicia and Manuel lived peacefully until one night, when they heard a loud, persistent knock on their front door at one o'clock in the morning: "We told ourselves that this time they were going to take us. Manuel went to open the door; it was the policeman from the house next door. He came to tell us: 'A search warrant arrived at the police station for both of you, and they're coming for you tomorrow and taking you to the Third Army Corps.' This guy was taking a big gamble because we had nothing in common, other than the fact that we were neighbors, though good neighbors. We packed our bags and got into the Citroën and we left without knowing where we were headed" (Ibid.). Military intelligence officers had found Alicia and Manuel again and then General Menéndez of the Third Army Corps had dispatched orders to disappear them. The police allowed the military to conduct their death squad operations, and were therefore often notified of an impending disappearance. So when their neighbor first saw the list of names of guerrillas, nothing immediately caught his attention—until he recognized the address of the house next door to his. He waited until his shift was over and, still wearing his uniform, knocked on their door. Stories of neighbors helping survivors after their release were somewhat common; it was far less common to hear stories of neighbors helping victims avoid being disappeared in the first place—especially when the neighbor was a police officer himself.

As soon as the police officer left, Alicia—who was pregnant—and Manuel packed as much as they could, along with their two kids, into their little Citroën that same night and drove until they reached Rosario, where Alicia's parents lived. Even though they were putting Alicia's parents at risk, they had nowhere else to go. While they were in Rosario, however, someone from Alicia's childhood, who now worked for the military, reported sighting Alicia to the Second Army Corps. This was the unpredictability of dictatorship-era Argentina: a police officer who found out that his next-door neighbors had been living under false identities helped them to escape, and a childhood acquaintance decided to turn the same family in.

A group of men went looking for Alicia and Manuel at her parents' house. The security forces abused and threatened her parents, trying to force them to reveal Alicia's location. Her parents claimed to know nothing, and in response, the men threatened to kill Alicia's sister. Alicia's

parents refused to trade one daughter in for another. Since Alicia and Manuel were not living with her parents, Alicia had no knowledge of what had
happened. The following day, her parents' neighbor called Alicia to inform
her that she was being hunted. Alicia immediately severed all contact with her
family and moved to a convent in Córdoba. Manuel's parents were close
with the nuns, who agreed to hide Manuel and his family. By this time it
was 1980, and Alicia's third child, Pablo, had been born.

Alicia and Manuel miraculously escaped the same fate as the compañeros around them, in large part because of their well-connected families,
who could provide not only financial support, but also social connections
that allowed them to survive. When the dictatorship ended in 1983, Alicia
and Manuel moved out of the convent, but remained in Córdoba. While they
managed to escape being disappeared, Alicia and Manuel had been leading
a life completely detached from friends and family under false identities.

When they reentered society, they had absolutely no social support.
Alicia remembered her neighbors were suspicious of them because their
long absence was seen as proof of their guilt. After her interview, Alicia said
that her relationship with Ceci had been strained over the years, because
of the trauma Ceci suffered from having been separated from her parents
when she was young. For Alicia, her time in internal exile was the harshest
effect of state terrorism, but this aspect of being a political prisoner went
unrecognized. Internal exile was another form of disappearance—they had
to disappear themselves, to disengage with the world, in order to survive.
When they came out of hiding, there was no acknowledgment of what they
had suffered.

Similarly, AEPPC member Américo Aspitia, who was detained in 1974
and 1975, before the dictatorship, for his labor union activities, and then
kidnapped again during the dictatorship, in 1976, spoke about the hard-
ships of internal exile in his interview: "The consequences of internal exile
are worse in your own country because when you go to another country,
they treat you better there. Here, if they found out that I was a political
prisoner, they'd start to cut my face. In your own country! It's twice as bad.
Who studies this? Who has studied cultural banishment? What psychologist understands these types of problems? Who could treat me from this
psychological point of view? Losing my home because they wouldn't let me
live in my own house?" (Aspitia, April 2009).

Though the effects of having once lived in exile are hard to track in con-crete terms, ex-presos, like Américo, felt that those exiled within Argentina were not seen to have suffered as much as those who lived in exile outside of the country. Juan Villa, who lived in internal exile for three years, said that he literally hid inside a basement. "I never went outside," said Juan. To ensure his safety, Juan "did not speak to anyone, watch television, or even listen to the radio" (Villa, May 209). Ex-presos view internal exile as an example of state terrorism because it was the threat of being disappeared that forced ex-presos to live underground. Their periods of internal exile added to the challenges of being able to reintegrate back into society—for both those who were eventually imprisoned during the dictatorship, and for those who remained hidden until the dictatorship lost power.

Broken Partnerships

More than half of the people who were disappeared and imprisoned dur-ing the dictatorship were in their teens or twenties, a time when they were still attending school, starting their first jobs, getting married, or having children. The torture and imprisonment that these youths endured would impact their lives over time, particularly because it happened when they were just becoming adults. "We were so young. We were taken during the time when we were discovering who we were, when we were figuring out our careers, starting families, and developing into adults. The damage we suffered is because of what happened to us, at that critical age," said AEPPC member Ester Cabral (personal conversation, July 20, 2008). Ex-presos spoke about unfinished college degrees, broken relationships, and dismantled political organizations that had once defined them. Released prisoners found many of their personal relationships with neighbors, friends, families, and spouses changed upon their return. Imprisonment disrupted and irreversibly changed people's life courses. More specifically, being imprisoned caused people to miss opportunities—many kinds of opportunities that cannot be easily measured. For example, even if both members of a couple were disappeared, one might survive and the other might not, or both might survive but come out different people. Imprison-ment changed people's lives so much that this type of loss left an imprint on the rest of their lives.

Within the AEPPC, there are few married couples; at the time of my research, most members were single, living with their second partner, or widowed. "Many compañeros separated from their spouses, and they couldn't incorporate themselves into the larger social struggle and were left marginalized, and now they find themselves living in the worst circumstances," said AEPPC member Sara Liliana Waitman (Waitman, August 2008). The majority of the members were not friends with each other prior to joining the AEPPC, but some had met before or in prison. Through informal conversations, I heard some of the stories of the ex-presos before they were abducted. One particular case dramatically illustrates the enduring effects a major disruptive event can have on individual lives. This is the story of Gladys Regalado and Rodolfo "Petiso" Novillo.

"I Was Saved from Marriage!"

Gladys Regalado works at the Archivo, and I visited her almost daily to socialize and to review what had been said at the previous AEPPC meeting. She has a sweet tooth and a penchant for cigarettes, and I would often share sweetbreads with her over mate that she prepared with hefty amounts of sugar. Before interviewing her, I already knew that Gladys was a widow and had three children. Her husband, who had not been a prisoner, had died when their children were still young. I also knew that, while Gladys had several siblings, only she and her older brother, Roberto, were politically involved during their youth. Roberto's wife, María del Carmen, "Mariela," was also politically active. All three were part of the PRT. The interview took place in the Archivo's library when work was particularly slow. Gladys spoke at length about the day she fell into the hands of the military.

At the time Gladys was abducted, she was not married and had not yet met the man she would later marry; in fact, she was about to marry someone else, Petiso ("Shorty"), a fellow militant and friend of her brother's. They had fallen in love while being active in the PRT movement and began living together. When she was twenty years old, they decided to get married. Petiso and Gladys set their wedding for June 28, 1977, and in preparation they went to the civil registrar to file their marriage certificate. They also had premarital blood tests one morning, to ensure that neither had any genetic or health problems, and planned to spend the rest of the afternoon at Roberto's house. It was June 22—six days before their wedding was supposed to take place.

On their walk back, the military closed in on them:

We didn't get married on June 28. They detained us on the twenty-second. That day we had gone to do our analysis. We had everything ready, with the date and everything set to get married on the 28th day of June. I remember we were going to talk on the phone with Petiso's mom, to tell her that everything was done for the wedding. And they detained us in the street. It would have been about a quarter to seven in the afternoon. We were walking down the avenue, and all of a sudden we heard a car braking and civilians jumping out running. They put guns to our heads. They put us against the wall, and someone from the car, a woman said, "It's Petiso Novillo." They blindfolded us. They put us in different cars. . . . They took me to La Perla. . . . I remember that I saw Petiso, that they put him in the stable.[2] The space was bigger than I realized. When they opened the door to the stable, I saw that there were a lot of prisoners inside. They took me to another room that was much smaller that also had prisoners. Then they took me to the interrogation room. (Regalado, September 2008)

Both Gladys and Petiso were held at La Perla, and, soon after, the military forcibly took Gladys with them to disappear her brother Roberto and his wife, Mariela. They were all taken back to La Perla, where they were held blindfolded. Eventually, Gladys was transferred to another concentration camp; La Ribera, and her brother and Mariela were also transferred there later:

I coughed so that they would realize that I was there until a guard took me to another room. They had me cross the patio and took me to a bigger room. I felt that there was someone else in that room. They put me in there, and they locked me in. I coughed. The other person coughed, and it was my sister-in-law. She said, "Gladys?"

"Yes, Mariela, it's me."

"What are you doing here?" We cried. We figured that someone was listening to us. The only thing that my sister-in-law did was cry

a lot, and said to me, "Now, they are going to kill us. We're not getting out of here. They are going to kill us." This is all she would say
to me.

I said, "Let's not talk because that's probably why they put us
together." (Ibid.)

When families and compañeros were brought into camps together, it
was usually for the purpose of interrogation sessions, where they tortured
one person to force another to speak:

After they took us to a room where the prisoners were, they put
us on a mattress. I don't remember what the mattress was made
of. I knew that we were all there on the floor, sitting single file.
Later, I found out Petiso was brought to La Ribera. I don't remember for how many days. My brother was there together with Petiso
in the other room because the women were in one and the men in
the other at La Ribera. Then came the interrogators; they took you
at night. They tortured all the compañeros—the crying, the pain. I
remember the night that they performed a mock execution. They
took us out at three in the morning. They told us to get into formation. They told us to face the wall in the patio of La Ribera. We heard
them say, "Prepare your guns. Load your guns." And you heard them
loading their guns. And then you start thinking about everything. It
was a split second, and then they kill you. They all started to laugh.
They got us back in single file again. (Ibid.)

At no time did Gladys, or any other prisoner, have any way of knowing
whether they were going to live or die during one of the torture sessions
or in one of the mock executions. Some compañeros died under torture;
some groups of prisoners never returned: "They took my sister-in-law one
day. I heard them take my brother and Petiso also. I asked where they were
and they told me to stay calm, that they had killed all three. In about fifteen
days my sister-in-law returned. All three returned. They had taken them to
La Perla. I hadn't returned to La Perla. They were in La Perla for quite a few
days. I was always in La Ribera, until one good day, they called my sister-in-
law and me. To the two of us, they said, "You're going to prison" (Ibid.).

Gladys said the transfer was a positive sign because they were being moved from La Ribera to UP1, a regular prison where they would have a greater chance of survival. From UP1, Gladys would eventually be transferred to Villa Devoto. When I asked her about her release, and how she felt about her freedom, she said: "My compañeras could not say good-bye or else they would be punished. So I yelled to them that the most beautiful people I had ever known were behind bars. They didn't answer me. I loved them a lot. I was in bad shape when I left. I left behind my sister-in-law too. After I left, I went through a rough period"(Ibid.). Several compañeros reported feeling sadness, loneliness, guilt, and unhappiness when they were released because they had left behind an entire community of compañeros. The military gave no reason why certain people were freed nor why at that particular time. Even three decades after the end of the military dictatorship, the ex-presos still do not have any more answers than they did then.

Gladys was released on her birthday, January 23, 1979. One of her brothers had come to Buenos Aires to pick her up and to bring her back to Córdoba; the trip was terrifying for Gladys. She was frightened of being abandoned and kidnapped again by the military. She remembered that her brother had to use the bathroom before they got on the train, and she was too frightened to be left alone and paranoid of being kidnapped, so she stood by the entrance of the men's bathroom. Her fear did not subside, even when her family—and Petiso's family—all came and greeted her at the train station when she arrived in Córdoba. But one week after her release, she got on a train and traveled to La Plata to visit Petiso and her brother, Roberto, at Unidad 9 de La Plata (Prison Unit 9 of La Plata, or U9), the men's prison in the province of Buenos Aires.

While her family was able to get together, have fun, dance, and laugh, she could not."I did everything to look content but I couldn't bring myself to join them. I stayed sitting, because I felt bad" (Ibid.). This depression prompted her family to look for ways to help Gladys:

One day my sister—it had been already a few months—said to me, "Nothing makes you happy. What's wrong? You spend all day being bitter." So then they started to pressure me. He started to visit me, the one who became my husband. He was interested in me.

But before, it was Petiso; we had been engaged. And when this guy knew that I had been released, he came looking for me—he knew the whole history of Petiso. And, well, we started a relationship. It was something that happened because I felt bad and I didn't want to feel so lonely, but the question was to tell Petiso. I traveled to La Plata to speak to Petiso and to tell him the truth. And I couldn't do it because my soul had left me. I had been completely in love. I finally wrote him a letter and I knew I was doing something shitty to Petiso. But afterward, I realized that all of this happened because of the pressure from my own family. I left him several times, my husband. And he cried. I went crying to my family, I cried by myself, and, well, then we got married while Petiso was still inside prison. When Petiso came out, my family still loved him very much. When he was freed, they organized a barbecue; it was his birthday. He asked my brother that I come, and we had our reunion, but I had gone with my husband and my son. I already had a son, but when we saw each other, we ran into each other's arms, to cry, to kiss each other. And we stayed like this that day. He came and visited my family, more with me. The only thing he said to me that day was, "This is the son that should have been mine." But later it was fine. He later married Pacha and formed a beautiful family. (Ibid.)

I asked Gladys if she was still in contact with Petiso and she said, "Yes, he works around the corner" (Ibid.). While I had been listening to her story, I had not realized that I actually already knew Petiso because I knew him as Rodolfo Novillo. The Archivo and the Municipal Office for Human Rights were both based in the same colonial-era building. In fact, although they worked for two different organizations, Gladys and Petiso worked a mere twenty paces from each other.

Petiso, or Rodolfo Novillo, is short and trim, and I was not surprised to learn that he came from one of the most well-regarded Argentine families—a part of the old elite. Although his family was divided politically, he described all of his siblings and parents as very close to one another, despite their ideological differences. Petiso is soft-spoken, an intellectual—when I met him, he was, at age fifty-one, working toward his graduate degree in history. (He had returned to school six years earlier, in 2002.) While he had studied history and political science at a university in his youth, his imprisonment and then his life after his release left little time and resources to continue his studies. Even without finishing his degree, he naturally looked the part of an academic—he favored fine-gauged sweaters and button-down shirts with khakis and usually carried a leather shoulder bag. He would occasionally make appearances at AEPPC meetings, listening, reflecting, and sharing his thoughts quietly after someone sought his opinion. At the municipality, he headed the Human Rights Office, primarily focusing on labor issues as well as social services. Because he was an historian, I often engaged him in long discussions about Perón, Nazism, and labor movements. Petiso was not as deeply involved in the AEPPC as the other compañeros, but he was always present for rallies, marches, and events connected to human rights issues, trials, and labor disputes.

I interviewed Petiso after I found out about his history with Gladys. I had already established independent relationships with each of them, but had never spoken about one to the other. After an hour of casual conversation, he began his story, and forty minutes into the interview, Petiso spoke about his sister, who is a desaparecida. She was pregnant when she was kidnapped, and it is believed that her child is one of the five hundred stolen grandchildren. I asked Petiso to recount his kidnapping, even though I had heard Gladys's version:

REBEKAH: You can start with 1975, but Gladys told me the story and about how you two were going to get married!

PETISO: Yes.

REBEKAH: So, I'd like to—

PETISO: I was saved! I was saved! I saved myself! [laughs] No. . . .

REBEKAH: I would like to hear your story, your perspective for this oral archive interview.

PETISO: Yes . . . look. Yes. No, look. . . . How to explain. In this moment . . . March 1975, let's say. I fell in a federal police prison.

REBEKAH: Alone?

PETISO: Yes, I think so. Soon after, I was released. It was an era of social change. I was part of the vanguard. At the time, I had a role in the Guevarista Youth, the PRT youth. After I left the federal prison, I decided

I needed to leave. I left and went to Italy. I was there for nine months in Italy.

REBEKAH: In what year?

PETISO: It was from May '75 to February '76.

REBEKAH: Did you like it?

PETISO: Two months before the coup I was doing activist work over there in Italy, in Rome, in Florence. (Novillo, September 2008)

Without having given me a direct answer, Petiso continued to talk for about an hour about the social, labor, and political movements around the world. He talked at length about the Cordobazo. He also talked more about his exile in Italy and his return to Argentina just before the last military dictatorship began in March of 1976, and he joked about being saved from marrying Gladys.

Later in the interview, I prompted him again to recall the day that he was kidnapped in 1977:

REBEKAH: You were with Gladys, no? When they took you?

PETISO: Yes, yes. . . . When I returned to the country, in the beginning of '76, when I met her, she was living in a house with another girl. Then came the coup. I went to stay at a friend's house in a neighborhood close to Gladys. This friend offered me protection and I stayed in her house. While living there, I met Gladys because she was living in the same neighborhood and had a brother who lived in front—he was a friend of mine, Gladys's brother. So, I met Gladys. (Ibid.)

Petiso said that the two of them spent an intense year together, and eventually he moved in with Gladys and her family. "It wasn't just a good relationship; she was also very much in solidarity with the movement," said Petiso (Ibid.). Then Petiso proceeded to recount the day they had gone to get tested for diseases before getting married:

PETISO: We were coming from the place where we got tested when they kidnapped us, because we had passed by the exact place where the people from La Perla, the military and civilian men, had been waiting for another person. That person they were waiting for was Gladys's sister-in-law, María del Carmen, who had been living with us. She had an appointment. The person she was supposed to meet for her appointment had fallen. So, they arrived there to wait for María del Carmen or that other person—I don't know who it was. When the group showed up, they immediately identified me. They knew who I was. I was on a capture list. Because I had left the country and came back, I had fake identification. But just that day, when I left the house with Gladys, I grabbed the fake ID from my bag and said, "No, wait a minute," and I left it behind. I left with my real ID. This ended up helping us. Because if I had been clearly walking around with a false document, and then was assaulted at La Perla, if the false ID was on me, then it's like, evidence that I was continuing to walk around—

REBEKAH: It was more suspicious—

PETISO: That's right. It was a little crazy to fall while carrying real identification papers; it's crazy! I only had the real ID on me because I was going to get married! It's the only reason I had it. Well, this is all speculation, you know? As for the question of saving myself from getting married—

REBEKAH: Are you serious?

PETISO: [Laughter] It saved me, I'm telling you, because I didn't marry Gladys. [Laughter]. After Gladys got out, she married someone else.

REBEKAH: Where were you afterward?

PETISO: Well, they kidnapped us; they grabbed us. They took us to La Perla. But they soon took Gladys to La Ribera. I stayed at La Perla for a month. Thirty days in La Perla.

REBEKAH: That's a long time.

PETISO: Yes, for me it was a long time. June 22 until July 22 in La Perla. (Ibid.)

Petiso also recalled being held at La Ribera before being sent to La Plata in October of 1978, where he was held until 1983. Petiso believed that they were helped by the fact that he wasn't carrying his false documents. The military already knew his real identity; if they found his false documents, they would have used them as evidence that he was a subversive, since it was against the law to carry false identification. Every Argentine citizen was expected to be able to show his or her identification at all times, but it was common practice for activists to assume false identities as a form of protection, using their noms de guerre, although Petiso cannot prove that his real documents helped their situation.

When Gladys was released in 1980, she waited for Petiso, but since many people were killed in prison and there was little certainty that she would see him again. Gladys ended up marrying another man out of family pressure. After Petiso was released from prison, he eventually married a woman named Patricia, or "Pacha," soon after his release. Pacha, a psychologist, already had two sons before marrying Petiso. He and Pacha had three daughters together. Their five children are all now in their twenties. Although Pacha, too, is an ex-presa, she does not attend AEPPC meetings.

In some ways, they had a happy ending: they each survived, got married, and had children—albeit not with each other. Gladys remarked that Petiso had a "beautiful family" even if they did not build one together. In 2008, they both were hard at work in the municipal offices of the Cabildo, maintaining their political activities and supporting the AEPPC. Gladys now works as the secretary for the Archivo, the part of the Cabildo that once operated as a CCD, and next door, in the same large and historic building, Petiso works in the municipal government's Office of Human Rights. Petiso was able to return to a university to finish his studies in history, almost three decades after he first started. Still, the military repression changed their lives: had they not been detained, they would have gotten married on June 28, 1977.

Meanwhile, for those involved in a relationship with someone who became a desaparecido, the relationship never had closure, because for several years, there was hope that a person would eventually be freed, or found. This was true for Sara Liliana Waitman's relationship with her boyfriend, Carlos "Nona" D'Ambra. (*Nona* means "granny" in Spanish.) "They called him Nona because he was young; he was twenty-three years old, and twenty-one when he studied physical education, but he already had gray hairs," said Sara (Waitman, August 2008). The military detained both of them at the Córdoba City bus station on November 20, 1976. Though Sara had been affiliated with the Communist Party, she was taken because she was with her boyfriend who was a PRT activist. They were on their way to visit his parents in Alta Gracia. Sara remembered her last conversation with Nona:

> The *verdes* [the greens, young military students] put us in a military truck and before they had us sit, they asked us for our documents. At that moment we didn't have our documents, and we waited about an

hour there sitting, and I asked Nona about the one who had boarded us. "He is a lieutenant junior grade," he told me. And I remember because he was bearded, fat, short, and spoke with a lisp. I will always remember this guy, his face, and the moment that we got on. Nona said to me, "Are you going to wait for me?" Because he had said, "Don't worry; you're going to get out quickly, but are you going to wait for me?" "Yes, my whole life, how am I not going to wait for you?" I said to him. I said these words with vigor, in a moment of absolute love. Without knowing at the time that in reality I was going to wait all my life, no? Because he became a desaparecido. (Ibid.)

Sara and Nona were abducted on a Saturday, and they were blindfolded and taken to La Ribera, where they were tortured. On Sunday, while still blindfolded, Sara was taken outside to the patio. Nona, who had seen her beneath his blindfold, began whistling "Zamba para olvidar (Zamba to forget)," an Argentine handkerchief dance song that the two of them enjoyed, as a way to tell her that he was there and, as Sara believes, to calm her. Sara was eventually transferred to UP1 and then to Villa Devoto, where she released from in 1979. After Nona was taken to La Perla, he was never seen again.

Sara later married a labor activist, Jorge, with whom she has a daughter. When I asked her if she still missed Nona, she said: "I remember when Jorge and I became a couple in '83, after democracy returned—because one always has hope that they can appear—a colleague of mine said, 'Sara, they said in the south, behind a lake, they are keeping the desaparecidos in a prison there.' I went and told Emi [Nona's mother]. 'No, Sara, they had already told us that,' she said. One always has hope, you know? There was hope that they would reappear after democracy returned" (Ibid.). Sara said that for a long time she had held onto the idea that one of the theories about the disappeared would turn out to be true: that they had left the country for security reasons or were hiding somewhere, and that when the dictatorship fell, they would all come back. "The memory of your first love always stays with you," said Sara (Ibid.).

Much has been written about this waiting period and the seemingly interminable mourning processes that people suffered through, without a body or a proper burial for closure (Bejarano 2002; Robben 2005; Bosco

2008). For Sara, letting go of Nona was difficult because she had promised to wait for him. The loss revolved around the lost potential of what Sara and Nona could have been as much as the actual physical loss of Nona. Sara continued to remember her disappeared boyfriend, Nona, even thirty years after his disappearance: "The figure of the desaparecido is something that causes pain and uncertainty. There's a constant search for things that you can never really know if they happened or not. In reality, you always keep wondering. At the current trial [against General Menéndez], people would still come up to me and ask about Nona. I'd say, 'I didn't see him,' and 'I didn't get to talk to him'" (Waitman, August 2008). Nona disappeared with Sara in 1976, and yet friends, compañeros, and family members were still asking Sara for details three decades later in 2008, during the trial against the former military officials responsible for the deaths at La Perla, wondering if there was anything new to learn.

Missed opportunities are not easily measurable when assessing the damage done to people's lives. Perhaps for this reason, in postwar or post–mass violence settings, the focus is on deaths—bodies can be counted—or perhaps on torture—scars can be measured. The loss of a potential future, however, is not considered a human rights violation to be compensated for in periods of transitional justice. The assumption that mere survival is enough falls short when considering the changes, losses, and ugly memories one must continue to face. Sara and others continue to live with the absence of their missing partners and with the lives they could have pursued with them.

Job Discrimination

Among the members of the AEPPC, the loss of labor opportunities is the most oft-cited long-term effect of imprisonment. In Argentina's first census of former political prisoners, conducted by the AEPPC in Córdoba Province between 2008 and 2009, 390 of the 550 former political prisoners surveyed had been working at the time they were detained. Fifty-nine percent of these people were either forced to quit or fired from their jobs after their release, and only 17 percent of them received severance pay (Gobierno de la Provincia de Córdoba, Secretaría de Derechos Humanos, September 28, 2009).

The reasons for unemployment are numerous. An ex-preso's over-all ability to work was constrained by the severe trauma experienced in prison. Ex-presos who wanted to work also faced discrimination because employers were fearful of hiring people who had been deemed subversive. Excluded from the formal sector, many ex-presos were forced to work *en negro* (under the table). Literally, this phrase means "in black," but it does not mean that the ex-presos worked in black market professions; they were simply not documented workers, even though they were all Argentine citizens. In addition to avoiding formal association with former political dissidents, employers did not have to provide the usual benefits and protections afforded to workers who were officially hired on the books. For the workers, this meant they had no recourse if they were wronged, and it also meant that they were not accruing any retirement savings. Ovidio Ramón "Pajarito" Ferreyra, who was imprisoned in 1975, for belonging to a labor union, described his job history this way: "At the moment I am working at the Secretariat of Human Rights, but until now I never could regain the social position that I had before they took me prisoner. Because I never could work legally, I was essentially marginalized, without health insurance, without the minimum benefits that any dignified person would have, and without the possibility of retirement, or medical attention or health insurance, or vacations, or any raise"(Ferreira, October 2008). Like Pajarito, many AEPPC members believe their present-day economic situation is a direct result of the job discrimination they faced after their release.

Many of the survivors who were formerly labor organizers, believe that their having to work without benefits stems from the dictatorship's efforts to eliminate the power of labor unions. The labor movement, which could have championed for benefits, suffered severe setbacks during the period of military repression. And the overall economic position of ex-presos was weakened because they were taken in their prime working years—their twenties—a period that would end up affecting the entire course of their lives.

As with many other dictatorial regimes, the bureaucracy was complicit in deciding who would succeed in the new political regime. There were no hard-and-fast rules or consistent bureaucratic practices such that all prisoners could follow a certain protocol to succeed in the formal economy. AEPPC member Jorge L. "Caballo" Argañaraz, who was imprisoned for his participation in a labor union, replied to my question on why some prisoners were considered to be more threatening than others. "We'll never know the psychology behind the system; only they [the military officials] know the categories and reasons for our imprisonment" (Argañaraz, September 2008). Until Argentina's government found secret documents on the persecution of specific individuals from the military dictatorship in November 2013, little was known about how the military categorized prisoners or whether evidence of blacklisting so-called subversives existed. According to these secret documents found in the basement of the air force headquarters, those blacklisted were turned down from jobs or forced into exile, and the military had a system of classifying individuals on a scale of F1 to F4 (Romero and Gilbert 2013). The F stood for formula and having a higher number meant that the person was more threatening. AEPPC members did not know what they were classified as, but these documents confirm the truth of their claims of job discrimination.

A Teacher Who Couldn't Teach Anymore

One of the ways in which former political prisoners encountered barriers to finding legitimate work was the mysterious lack of paperwork that could have restored them to their previous positions before they were imprisoned. Viviana "Vivi" Vergara was born in Córdoba in 1951, and was fifty-seven years old at the time I interviewed her on August 26, 2008. Vivi was generally quiet and rarely spoke in AEPPC meetings, though she chatted freely in our one-on-one interactions. Like most of the compañeros, Vivi is a chain smoker, and she often talked with her arms folded in front of her. She was divorced and had one son. Her mother's passing in 2008, took a heavy emotional toll, and she lost a considerable amount of weight. At the time of this research, Vivi was living with another AEPPC member, Enzo "Gringo" Sacco, and was often seen as his main supporter, particularly when he would get upset over debates in meetings. If he left in protest—which was fairly common as discussions often got heated—she would follow him out. I enjoyed watching the two of them together, both when I would run into them at local cafés, or when I would visit them at the Archivo while they worked on conducting the census of ex-presos. Vivi and Gringo would engage in lively discussions, often teasing one another, but always interspersing their jibes with obvious signs of affection. Whenever Gringo would give me a hard time for not sharing the extraordinary American wealth he was certain that I had, Vivi—who understood quite well the true economic position of a graduate student—would just sit back and smile, knowing that Gringo was only teasing me.

Vivi was arrested in 1977, for trying to unionize her bank colleagues. At the time, labor unions were outlawed. While her parents were Peronists, Vivi had no particular political affiliation. When she was released from prison in 1981, she faced tremendous difficulty finding new employment. Vivi already had her teaching credentials, but because she could not obtain a copy of her diploma after she was released from prison, she was barred from teaching. "The military disqualified you for life," said Vivi (Vergara, August 2008). When Vivi sought to make a new copy of her teaching certificate, the university told her that her records had been burned in the archive. Her twin sister, on the other hand, who had completed the same program and received the same degree, and had not been imprisoned, could still access a copy of her teaching credentials in the same exact archive.

Vivi, however, continued to pursue her teaching career in a different province, but she was unable to advance without the necessary paperwork. Fortunately, she was supported by her husband, who, like most of the ex-presos, was able to find work through a personal connection, but only en negro:

> I married another former prisoner who had gotten out in '82. He had gotten a job as a car salesman because he knew the car dealer. Then a better job came up in Rosario. We were already expecting a son, so we moved to Rosario with the hope that I could work there, because it was easier to get a job as a teacher in Rosario. Then after having worked as a teacher, I returned to Córdoba. I also separated from my husband not long after. I still have a very good relationship with my ex-husband, and will for my entire life. He is a good father and we're friends, but we separated for particular reasons. Each person has his own story of pain, and we fought, argued a lot, and, well, we ended up separating. By the time I returned to Córdoba, I was on my way to start working as a teacher. The thing that I didn't have

was the master's level and there wasn't a shortage of teachers, so I
didn't talk a lot about my past as a prisoner. (Ibid.)

Knowing that she could be discriminated against for being a political prisoner, Vivi did not speak openly about her past in order to keep her
job. She then began following the necessary steps to become a teacher in
Córdoba: "To work as a teacher you first had to work as a substitute. After
working as a substitute for several years, you earn your credential, except
if you choose to do a practicum. The interim posts for your practicum are
available all-year-round, and the positions for substitute teachers are available from March to December. During the other months, a lot of teachers
spent time at the administrative office to do their interim post" (Ibid.).

While Vivi worked at the administrative office, some colleagues
learned that she was an ex-presa. As a result, her salary was suddenly cut:

> It turned out that a teacher had mentioned that I had been impris-
> oned. I don't really know who had talked about me. I requested a
> leave for my studies. When I returned from my leave, they told me,
> "Good-bye, I hope you find another job as a substitute."
>   And I said, "What? I did a practicum."
>   "You didn't do any practicum," said the compañera who had
> reported to the director. The office director was against former
> political prisoners, and said that I had changed my practicum to do
> substitution work. And they cut off my salary. This was another kind
> of persecution, in the workplace. I kept struggling to reincorporate
> myself into society during the democratic period. (Ibid.)

Even when the state did not directly intervene, one's job security was
dependent on whoever was in charge and on that person's personal
beliefs and political opinions toward the dictatorship and the political prisoners. Because of situations like Vivi's, ex-presos often hid their
pasts and their former political affiliations in order to survive socially
and economically.

After being shut out from the teaching profession and denied her
old job at the bank, Vivi was eventually hired by the bank's labor union
because, while they could not reinstate her, they could hire her to conduct
labor activities. In this new job, when Vivi worked to prevent the closing of

the bank's health clinic, which was seen as too costly, the company forced her to voluntarily retire from her position. At this point she was not in the union; instead, she was hired on a contract basis. She said that despite all of the obstacles, she kept struggling to find work. She eventually got her master's degree and returned to substitute teaching for a brief period later in life. Over time, however, Vivi was not able to gain the full salary and benefits that went along with a permanent teaching position and that could have put her in a better financial position. Because of her tough economic situation, Vivi was one of a handful of AEPPC members nominated to work on the census. Ex-presos who did not have jobs, who were not in retirement, and faced financial difficulties were given first preference in filling the census work positions.

It's a Funny Story . . .

If Vivi's experience seemed exceptional, there were other official ways in which various employers could legally discriminate against former political prisoners. One concrete form of job discrimination that political prisoners faced had to do with presenting a police issued Certificado de Buena Conducta (Certificate of Good Conduct) as a requirement for work in the formal economy. This document certified that the applicant had no criminal record and was in good standing with the law. Fidel "Antonio" Alcázar, who was imprisoned for four years and eight months for being a sympathizer to resistance movements, was forced to work informally because his imprisonment appears on his Certificate of Good Conduct. As a result, Antonio "always worked as an independent contractor" because as the "third party outside of the official contract, no Certificate of Good Conduct was required" (Alcázar, October 2008).

Conversely, having a clean record could lead to steady work in the formal economy. At sixty-two, Élida "Ely" Eichenberger is one of the few members of the AEPPC who travels internationally. Having worked as a theater teacher at a Jewish school for decades, she enjoys the security of retirement benefits. She is also a writer, director, and teacher of biodanza.[3] During my fieldwork, she was in the middle of making two films, one of which is about the survivors of UP1, and she hopes to talk about collective memory through collective storytelling. The other film tells the story of a well-known Argentine family, the Pujadas, who were massacred by the Triple A for their leftist activities.

Born in the city of Esperanza in Santa Fe Province, once considered a German Swiss colony, Ely remembered her childhood fondly. She moved to the capital of Santa Fe to study film, and it was there that she said that she "discovered the world" (Eichenberger, October 2008). According to Ely, the particular film school she attended was considered to be a path into the Communist Party because the philosophy was to make either socially minded films, films that denounced societal ills, or social documentaries. For Ely, this was when she felt her "mind opened." It was also where she met her husband Paty "Pate" Ponze, with whom she had a daughter in 1967. And at the time, Ely did, in fact, become a member of both the Communist Party and the student council at her film school. But later, she disagreed with the party's politics and left. She briefly joined the Revolutionary Communist Party, but eventually left that as well. Instead, Ely became a PRT sympathizer, but not a militant within the organization, though Pate was a PRT activist.

After graduation, Ely began teaching classes at the university on social practice and conducting arts and theater with the broader community. But by 1974, the school fired her after the minister of national education, a fervent (right-wing) Peronist, removed those who belonged to the PRT as well as the Montoneros. Isabel Perón was in power, and it was during this time that the Triple A began killing political dissidents. Ely recalled her friend, Marta, a human rights lawyer, whose dead body was found floating in the river in her home province not long after the military abducted her. Marta's body had been beaten, burned with cigarettes, and had one breast cut off.

In 1975, Ely and her daughter decided to leave Santa Fe in order to avoid being taken by the military. Her husband accompanied her to the bus terminal and Ely begged him to come with them, but he refused, telling her that she was safe, and that they were more likely to come after him. Ely had only held public sector jobs, and, for this reason, she felt in some ways protected. As the bus was pulling away from the station, she saw a group of men close in on Pate through her window. Three days later, she found out that he had been executed.

Shortly after her husband's death, Ely returned to Santa Fe and opened a bookstore called The Elephant. On August 19, 1976, the military abducted

Ely. Many activists patronized her bookstore, and a younger activist had mistakenly believed that Ely was part of an activist operation and named her as a subversive. While her daughter was left to live with a neighbor, Ely was held in three different prisons and released from Villa Devoto at the end of 1979, under supervised release.

As part of the dictatorship's ideological regime, the military required that Ely attend classes on morality three times a week at the local police station in Alta Gracia—a small city in Córdoba Province where she was ordered to live. Ely did not recall the specific lessons; she remembered staying silent and nodding to whatever was said without giving any information about herself. Ely described the period of supervised release as particularly difficult: "When I got out, it didn't feel pleasurable, it didn't feel good to leave. Because . . . [pause] what followed was so ugly. Also, supervised release was really horrible as well. Because at least inside prison, you were with your compañeras, so everything was about working together to resist the military. In contrast, outside you were all alone, but you also knew that the military knew where you were at all times, and that they could find you at any moment" (Ibid.). When captives were taken to prison, they were divided into those who were *recuperable* (able to be rehabilitated) and those who were *irrecupable* (unable to be rehabilitated). Being labeled "irrecupable," however, did not necessarily mean execution or disappearance—some of the so-called irredeemable prisoners survived. But the distinctions established by the military did affect how people were treated in prison and during torture sessions, and how prisoners felt about their chances for survival. Nonetheless, the assumption was that prisoners who were released were considered recuperable, that they could be resocialized and turned into citizens who fit with the dictatorship's vision for the country.

Ely recounted how, with her Certificate of Good Conduct, she was able to find work as a teacher:

"When I went to find work in a school, I was told that they required that I submit a Certificate of Good Conduct. This was the funniest thing in the world. I was held under PEN [*Poder Ejecutivo Nacional*, or National Executive Authority] without a cause. As a result, I was considered to be extremely 'clean.' [laughs] About twenty days after I submitted my request, my Certificate of Good Conduct arrived while I was under house arrest. This was [the] craziest thing. I started to work in a school during the time I was in supervised release. Can you believe it?"(Ibid.).

Ely, who was granted a Certificate of Good Conduct despite having once been a Communist, found steady teaching jobs and was eventually hired by a Jewish day school. Because she worked, she was able to retire with a pension. Since then, she has traveled internationally and has returned to her original passion—filmmaking. Vivi, on the other hand, after a career of working mostly en negro, sometimes as a substitute teacher, continues to search for work. These two women are examples of how much impact residual bureaucratic practices could exert over one's reintegration into society.

The combination of not wanting to associate with political prisoners, and the lack of Certificates of Good Conduct, made it difficult for released prisoners to pursue work freely or to return to their previous places of employment. Political prisoners said that they had little or no choice but to accept jobs that were either outside of their intended field or without benefits. Retaining these jobs may not have been sufficient as they lived paycheck to paycheck as they resumed their lives. However, as they now reach retirement age, they face the dire consequences of never having been able to save for retirement. According to many political prisoners, their economic struggles at their advanced age are a constant reminder of the stigma that prevented them from finding more lucrative employment.

Family Strain

Imprisonment caused tremendous amount of stress on the families that were left behind. In some cases, political prisoners were able to receive a visit from their families once a year. These limited interactions with parents were heartening, but they were also painful and sources of stress because of the financial and emotional strain visiting placed on parents. At a public lecture at UCLA, on March 8, 2010, Irene Martínez, who was imprisoned while she was a medical student in Córdoba, remembered that after her father visited her in prison, he suffered a heart attack. Her mother, who made a separate visit to see her in prison, didn't appear as visibly distressed as her father had. Nevertheless, when she returned to her hotel room, Irene's mother fell down the stairs and broke her leg. Irene believes that these were physical reactions to the difficult experience of seeing her in prison.

Several ex-presos expressed guilt for having caused their parents grief and stress. Some, whose parents passed away during their imprisonment, felt that it was due to the tremendous amount of pain and stress they experienced having a disappeared child. Others felt guilty for simply not being there when a parent died. AEPPC member Cristina Correa, who was imprisoned for belonging to a labor union, said that that the single most difficult consequence of her imprisonment was living with the fact that she was not with her father when he died: "What affected me most was that a month before I was freed my father passed away and this had a tremendous impact on me" (Correa, September 2008). Other ex-presos interpreted a parent's death as a result of what had happened to them; they saw their arrests as exacerbating preexisting health conditions, or bringing health problems upon them through the stress and worry.

One of the questions included in the prompts for the oral history archive interviews was about reintegration into their family life after being released. AEPPC member Américo Aspitia, who had separated from his second wife because she came from a military family, said, "She went away with her father who was in the military. Her father was a retired air force commander. The dad got his daughter and took her away and they disappeared from my life. I never knew heard from her again" (Aspitia, April 2009). What Américo did not know, however, was that his wife was pregnant at the time they separated. She had given birth to a girl, and Américo did not meet her until 1998:

> My friend called me and said, "Hey, I have a person I want you to meet." He was a former political prisoner who was held in UP1 at the same time I was, named Huguito Basso. Huguito Basso called me and said, "Look, I want to see you."
>
> I said, "Well, I'm in Córdoba; come visit." I am cutting the story short.

He said, "Well, I'm bringing a person with me who wants to meet you." I thought that he had a fugitive with him, someone we hadn't seen in a long time. He arrived that same day at my house in a car with a girl.

I see the girl and say, "Hello."

She introduces herself, and Hugo says, "How is your heart? Are you doing well?" I haven't seen this guy Hugo Basso in years. But soon, we were just two old guys drinking beer, the three of us hanging out. I thought she was his girlfriend. And he says to me, "Your heart is good?"

"Look, I'm more or less good; I am under treatment."

"Ah, well, but you're good; I'm going to deliver some news to you then," he says. "It's pretty crazy, pretty crazy." Then he tells the girl, "Tell him your name."

And it was my daughter. When she told me her name, my heart almost broke. I looked at her.

"Are you absolutely sure about this? So, you meet your daughter after thirty years? Why are you doing this to me?" Then I said to him, "Why are you doing this Hugo, son of a bitch?" [laughing] And well, I can't narrate this moment; I never internalized it. I don't know what happened; my whole life story passed in a second, to see this woman who was twenty-two years old, now thirty-three. (Ibid.)

When América's second wife left Argentina, she never told their daughter about her father. But when América's daughter came back to Córdoba to visit, she began asking questions, and through Hugo she found América. She returned two days later, and they continue to write to each other, but América said that it continues to be a very difficult process: "It's very difficult for her, and it's very difficult for me. It's a really big deal. But had we been able to lead a normal life. . . . If life could have turned out like we planned. . . . We wanted to create political change in our country, to make it better. We didn't want them to kill us, to disappear us. Maybe she could have had a father this whole time. It wasn't us that brought this about. It was the others that provoked this" (Ibid.).

This statement made by Américo captures how ex-presos view state terrorism as the reason for, or instigator of, the struggles they faced. If, as Américo suggests, the dictatorship hadn't disappeared political activists and waged a war against them, then he and others could have led normal lives. In his case, Américo could have had a relationship with his daughter, but it was state violence that led to their separation. Still, Américo did feel that it was his responsibility for having lost out on his daughter's childhood. "I owe a big debt to my daughter that I am never going to settle," said Américo (Ibid.).

AEPPC member, Luís Acosta, who was kidnapped in 1976, for being a Montonero, believed that his imprisonment impacted the way in which he raised his children. "I had lost out on the first two or three years of my daughter's life, that for sure, certain behaviors of mine as a father are influenced by those years" (November 2008). Before speaking about the past, Luís thought nothing of his parenting style. But then he realized that his parenting was a reaction to his forced separation from his children. Luís said that his eldest child, who was a newborn when he was detained, was already three years old when he returned from prison. He had to learn at that point how to be a father to a child who had grown up in his absence. Luís said that his children became independent from an early age and moved out at twenty, twenty-one, and twenty-two years of age—something that he said was unusual in Argentina, where children often live at home into their thirties. Luís explained, "I needed them to be able to do things themselves, as if I always imagined them to be without parents, since they were little" (Ibid.). Luís found upon further introspection that his childrearing methods, which at first glance appeared to be a matter of personal preferences, were influenced by his absence during his imprisonment. Paranoid that he could be taken and separated from his children again, Luis felt the best way to prepare his children as a father was to make them independent, so that in the event he was absent, they would survive without him. For Luis, then, a pension would need not simply to compensate for the fact that he never finished an economics degree that could have potentially increased his earning power, but also to recognize that he suffered from effects of state terrorism that have impacted his family life in myriad subtle, yet powerful, ways.

Pensions for Early Death?

The stigma attached to imprisonment continued to negatively affect ex-presos' ability to rebuild their lives outside of prison, even during periods of democratic rule. Ex-presos' struggles with family life, the silence surrounding their exile, and lack of legitimate employment, all characterize the mundane ways in which the legacies of state terrorism impacted their lives. In other words, ex-presos view their everyday personal struggles as a consequence of state repression, and it is the culmination of these daily struggles over the course of their lives that is most significant. AEPPC members believe that cumulative effects of state terrorism and its aftermath have translated into early death.

During my time in Argentina, if an ex-preso heard that another compañero had died or was diagnosed with a terminal illness, they would often comment that it was due to the effects of state terrorism. When making this comment, ex-presos would raise their eyebrows at me as if to say, "Take note; this is proof." On numerous occasions, ex-presos told me that their own health and financial problems were a direct (albeit belated) result of state terrorism. The 2008 census of ex-presos in Córdoba Province found that approximately eight out of ten suffer from sicknesses or physical disorders, and three out of ten had some kind of psychological illness (Gobierno de la Provincia de Córdoba, Secretaría de Derechos Humanos, September 28, 2009). In addition, the majority of the 324 ex-presos who identified themselves as being ill, reported that their health problems stemmed from the violence they experienced under the dictatorship (Ibid.).

In the time since I left the field, three of the AEPPC members I interviewed, died from chronic health diseases that their compañeros link to the trauma they experienced earlier in life. Atilio Basso died on March 16, 2010, from heart failure; Víctor Eduardo Ferraro passed away from lung cancer on January 3, 2011; and Luís Acosta also died of lung cancer on May 10, 2011. Two ex-presos who were major figures in the human rights movement and frequent fixtures at AEPPC events in Córdoba have also since passed away: Richard Scalet, president of the National Organization of Ex-Presos, on March 13, 2013, and María Elba Martínez, a human rights lawyer, on August 18, 2013. The number of deaths of ex-presos in the AEPPC network is so alarming that the ex-presos began collecting data in

May 2011, on those who had recently passed away and their cause of death. Collecting reports from around Córdoba Province, where approximately 1,200 ex-presos live, AEPPC member Sara Liliana Waitman counted 62 ex-presos who were between the ages of 55 and 62 when they died, many of them from cancer or from heart-related health problems.[4] The surviving members of the AEPPC are concerned that those around them—and perhaps they themselves—will pass away at equally early ages, and, they worry, at an increasingly rapid pace.

In working with ex-presos and with families of the disappeared, Argentine psychiatrist Dr. Luis Jorge Damonte, who is also an ex-preso, found a range of health problems among survivors of state terrorism:

> The concrete manifestations of what had happened in the past are anxiety disorder and panic attacks—anxiety disorder is when an individual starts to have symptoms where they feel nervous and feel like something terrible is going to happen to them. They can't finish what they had been doing. All of these symptoms generate psychiatric anguish that is translated into various forms of trauma in their bodies, manifested in illnesses like gastritis, cardiovascular problems, kidney-related diseases, heart attacks, and high-blood pressure (because it can be fatal). Other somatizations include not being able to carry out the same activities that one was doing before, panic attacks where you suddenly can't be in a certain place because you remember what had happened to you. (translation from author, http://www.elmorterodigital.com.ar/node/163, accessed August 1, 2013)

Rather than speaking about the specific health problems they suffered, ex-presos spoke in their interviews about the social and economic impacts of having been imprisoned. Imprisonment kept them from their families. Labeling them as subversives and as terrorists fueled the public perception that ex-presos not only deserved what happened to them, but that they should also be shunned after their release from prison. These mundane struggles then manifested themselves through bodily illnesses. For these reasons, ex-presos have demanded more reparations.

Throughout the 1990s, ex-presos had received compensation for denied income they could have earned had they not been in prison. On

November 27, 1991, the National Congress passed Law 24.043, which mandated that victims of arbitrary detentions between November 6, 1974 and December 10, 1983, were paid in bonds with $74 (in U.S. dollars) face value for each day of detention (Guembe 2006, 31). However, the government did not start paying reparations to approximately 7,800 petitioners until 1994 (Ibid.).

Thus, the amount of money an ex-preso received was determined by how many days they were imprisoned. However, ex-presos do not believe this reparation amount was enough, financially or morally. First, the fact that these reparations were paid in bonds meant that ex-presos did not receive the full amount that they were entitled to; many were forced to cash in their bonds before they matured, due to economic struggles. In addition, the 2001 economic collapse, in which the value of the Argentine peso plummeted, severely reduced the value of the bonds. To illustrate how ex-presos received less than they were owed, let us consider what happened to one of the AEPPC members, "Agustín.[5]" In 1994, the Ministry of the Interior awarded Agustín $63,237.02 worth of Argentine sovereign bonds in compensation for 847 days of detention. Because Menem had pegged the peso to the dollar in 1991, the bonds could be issued either in U.S. dollars or in Argentine pesos. Agustín reported that he would have had to wait seven years—not sixteen, as Maria José Guembe (Guembe 2006, 33) reported—for the bonds to mature.

But like other ex-presos, who came out of prison jobless, often with families to support, or in similarly dire financial situations, Agustín could not wait, and decided to sell his bonds at market rate. He put his bonds in a *caja de valores* (securities depository), which charged a brokerage fee of $7,489, immediately reducing the value of his bonds to $55,748. Agustín instructed the brokers to sell the bonds at four different points during 1994. The first time, he sold $15,748 worth of bonds at a rate of about 67 percent, and received $10,580.21. The second time, $7,000 was exchanged at the rate of 65 percent, netting him $4,585. The third time, $3,000 was exchanged at 66.5 percent, giving this ex-preso $1,995. The fourth and final time Agustín sold bonds, he received $19,532 after selling the remaining $30,000 worth at about 65.5 percent. In the end, Agustín recovered only $36,692 from the bonds, meaning that he lost out on $26,545 of the total amount the state owed. Those who did wait seven years, ironically, received the least of all, because Argentina's 2001 economic collapse sent the value of their bonds plummeting to about 50 percent of their original value.

The second reason why ex-presos did not see the first set of reparations as sufficient is because it did not compensate them for all that they have suffered, not just torture but also the legacies of state terrorism. "We had economic compensation for the years we spent in prison, but we do not consider it just, because the harms done went beyond the material," said AEPPC member Manuel Nieva (September 2008). Another AEPPC member, Hugo "Gato" Ferrandans, said: "The indemnity served as a stop-gap for urgent needs, but it didn't help me to recover my life. Life for the majority of us never returned to a sense of normal. We were never normal people again" (May 2009). The combination of these two reasons was the main impetus behind ex-presos organizing themselves on a national level to demand another set of reparations in 2009.

Toward the end of my fieldwork, the national group of ex-presos had decided to petition for reparations on a province-by-province basis to quicken their results, while simultaneously pushing for a national law. Specifically, they requested retirement pensions, and the immediacy of such money was emphasized by their age and by the shared perception both that their compañeros were dying earlier than average and that they were all at risk for dying early because of what had happened to them. In 2010, Córdoba Province granted a monthly subsidy to ex-presos who were arrested between 1976 and 1983, and did not already receive retirement benefits. Unsatisfied with the legislation, the AEPPC continues to lobby the provincial government to provide subsidies to all ex-presos who fell starting in 1974, and to administer them not as a form of poverty alleviation, but as recognition of victims of state terrorism. Congress approved a national subsidy law for former political prisoners in November 2013, though as of this writing, the subsidy had yet to be distributed.

Returning to the image of the rupture that Veena Das employs to speak about ordinary forms of suffering, I have argued in this chapter that ex-presos believe that the legacies of their imprisonment had long-lasting impacts upon their lives. After they were released from prison, they still felt oppressed because they had to comply with military orders of where to live and how to behave in the recuperation process. Being forced to hide and to hide their pasts, in addition to dealing with memories of torture and prison life, made everyday living a constant struggle. These struggles, ex-presos believe, should also count as human rights violations. Because they were victims of state terrorism, their lives were effectively destroyed even if they survived the camps. The question of what counts as a violation matters not only in acknowledging how the ex-presos view their own experiences in the aftermath of the dictatorship, but also in determining what qualifies a person for financial reparation. The AEPPC and other groups of ex-presos have demanded, and continue to demand, further reparations for the damages they suffered as a result of lingering effects that state terrorism left behind.

6

Post-Transitional Justice

Who counts as a victim and what counts as a violation are questions that determine how former political prisoners in Córdoba view the success of transitional justice measures. Legal and human rights scholars have regarded all that Argentina accomplished soon after the dictatorship ended—the truth commission, the historic Trial of the Juntas, and reparations—as evidence of a successful transitional justice process (Arthur 2009; Faulk 2012). Yet, the ex-presos remain dissatisfied with what the state had failed to do for survivors of state terrorism until recently. Ex-presos started organizing in the mid-2000s, in response to their economic and health problems and are, as of this writing, continuing to lobby for reparations, which suggests a new era of post-transitional justice (Skaar 2011)—one that continues to seek remedies for the legacies of crimes committed during the dictatorship.

One of the central themes raised in this research with former political prisoners is the uncomfortable question of their survival: why did the military choose them and not others to live? When the political prisoners were released, the human rights community—which was primarily made up of the kin of the desaparecidos—did not immediately embrace them, and instead blamed them for the continued disappearance of loved ones. Suspicion arose around the silences in ex-presos' testimonies of the events that happened in the CCDs. These silences, as the accusation goes, may have revealed the survivors' guilt in compromising the lives of others in exchange for their own survival. Thus, their status as traitors highlighted the fact that not all victims of the dictatorship were treated the same by human rights groups. Desaparecidos were seen first as innocent victims, and later as heroes of the leftist movements. Meanwhile, the reappeared, the ex-presos, were seen as failing to give themselves over to the revolutionary dream, which their disappeared compatriots had accomplished through their deaths. Outside of the human rights movement, the ex-presos continued to be seen as terrorists for their identities as political activists. The phrase, "For some reason they were taken," was said during the dictatorship to justify turning away from those who had disappeared, and it was only reinforced in the post-dictatorship era by the continued marginalization of the reappeared desaparecidos.

I focus on the dual victimization of having been first disappeared and then later marginalized because it demonstrates that not only did ex-presos suffer from torture and degrading prison conditions, but they also faced discrimination as a result of those initial human rights violations. My intention in writing about the 2007 formation of the AEPPC was to illustrate how their lack of victim status deprived them of a place within the early human rights landscape among the kin-based groups in Argentina. I argue that increasing the presence of ex-presos at memorialized sites and circulating their memories of their activism widens the dialogue beyond torture. Furthermore, it opens discussions on both the political motivations behind activism, and the moral choices one encounters in the *gray zone*, to borrow Primo Levi's term, in *The Drowned and the Saved* (Levi 1989 [1986]). The dual presence of the disappeared and the reappeared, in this case the ex-presos, invites discussion on why revolutionary movements were seen as the only option to create social change, and what could have taken place instead of disappearances to resolve political differences. These dialogues, I suggest, may serve to lessen the stigmatization of ex-presos.

Yet the ex-presos have struggled to determine when, where, what, and how they are able to speak about the past. The challenge is not simply to gain the status of victims of human rights violations, but also to inhabit the role of tour guide in memorial museums in order to circulate memories of activism in prison, rather than of torture. The AEPPC members are invested in telling stories of resistance and solidarity because such accounts speak to their survival and reflect the way in which they want to teach youths about their role in recent Argentine history. In the last decade, as the political context has changed in favor of human rights more generally, the ex-presos have become more visible, and more nuanced understandings of the past have made it possible to look more positively on those who participated in social movements during the last dictatorship. Still, more work needs to be done in recovering the memories of the ex-presos; their participation is a recent phenomenon.

Drawing more scholarly attention to the history and views of ex-presos in Argentina is an urgent task. Several compañeros have already passed away, and many currently living ex-presos fear early deaths. If the task of instructing new generations on the survivors' version of history has any chance of continuing after the main protagonists are gone, then their memories must be recorded sooner rather than later. For example, this research produced the AEPPC's first oral history archive, which has become valuable precisely because it includes recordings of interviews with three recently deceased ex-presos: Luís Acosta, Atilio Basso, and Víctor Eduardo Ferraro. These are the only recorded interviews that these three ex-presos ever made. The Archivo is also in the process of producing a video archive of survivors, but for the compañeros who died before having the opportunity to record their stories, it is already too late.

While most of what I have written focuses on the connections between the ex-presos' identity, the changing political context, and commonly circulated memories, I have also brought attention to the economic and social discrimination that ex-presos experienced since their release from prison. Even after the return to democracy, the stigma attached to dictatorship-era imprisonment severely limited their life projects and continued to affect them over time. While it may be torture that defines the ex-presos as victims, the types of violations that the ex-presos identified as most detrimental were the secondary effects of torture and imprisonment. These negative consequences included broken relationships, lost time, failed careers, and forced silence. By describing the mundane ways in which the ex-presos have suffered, I set the context so as to understand why the political prisoners are demanding a new round of pensions to compensate for having been tortured and victimized by state terrorism. Ex-presos want recognition for the suffering they have endured during democracy.

It is precisely because the ex-presos were not defined as victims in the early post-dictatorship era, and because they were subjected to social discrimination for having once been imprisoned, that AEPPC members believe the early transitional justice efforts ignored their needs as survivors of state terrorism. But they do, however, believe that the past decade has seen changing public attitudes toward former activists in the dictatorship era, and political leadership that leans to the left. When asked, "What has been the most important effort that the state has undertaken that has helped survivors?" twenty-two of the political prisoners said, "*los Kirchners*," referring to former president Néstor Kirchner and his successor and wife, Cristina Fernández de Kirchner, the current president of Argentina. This response revealed my mistake: I wanted to evaluate specific transitional justice measures, rather than the moment in which ex-presos believed that there were possibilities for justice. The normative environment had changed in Argentina so that certain human rights abuses were no longer seen as acceptable—namely disappearances—and this change in public attitude reflected a more receptive political climate toward those victimized by the military dictatorship. Kathryn Sikkink's concept of the "justice cascade," in *The Justice Cascade: How Human Rights Prosecutions Are Changing World Politics* is instructive here: "a shift in the *legitimacy of the norm* of individual criminal accountability for human rights violations and an increase in criminal prosecutions on behalf of that norm" (Sikkink 2011, 5, emphasis in the original). Sikkink, while focusing specifically on legal measures, draws a connection between changing social norms and the feasibility of achieving legal measures because of the new norms. Though many of the ex-presos certainly confirmed Sikkink's theory, their answer also extended beyond the topic of justice.

The answer, los Kirchner, refers to several things. Mainly, it is about the fact that the Kirchners have helped change societal norms about human rights. Juan Carlos Álvarez said, "What the Kirchners' governments have done is made human rights policy a central issue, as the basis of state policies, something that previous governments have not done" (Álvarez, February 2009). When pressed to be more specific about what exactly los Kirchners did for human rights, Rodolfo "Petiso" Novillo, said, "It's about the fact that the Kirchner government had contributed to, not as the primary author, but contributed to establishing questions of human rights as a state matter" (Novillo, September 2008). For example, Petiso said the state took charge of matters related to "youth, labor, health, housing, and employment" (Ibid.). To give a more concrete example of how human rights became institutionalized, Alicia Staps said: "We have received government support on the national, provincial, and municipal level where we have secretariats and offices of human rights, not just for victims of state terrorism, but for much more than that. The Secretariat of Human Rights in Córdoba, the one doing the census on political prisoners in order to create a reparation policies, has an office for sexual discrimination, one for the handicapped, one for the unemployed, and so on"(Staps, November 2008). For the majority of the ex-presos interviewed, the Kirchners ushered in a new era of human rights in which it became a regular state-related affair. The Kirchners are considered to have changed public attitudes about the importance of observing and ensuring basic human rights.

Second, the establishment of human rights as a state matter meant that the Kirchners also took specific measures to ensure justice. "President Kirchner is the one who opened the door to human rights," said Gladys Regalado. "I believe his government opened the door for us so that today we could bring the genocidaires to justice, so that now we have Menéndez in prison for life" (Regalado, September 2008). The current success in bringing former military officials trials is attributed to Kirchner, because of the steps he had to take for the trials to resume. "The annulment of the impunity laws encouraged our society to settle accounts. The most important thing for the survivors is that they see justice done," said Atilio Basso (Basso, October 2008). Kirchner replaced the judges on the Supreme Court and nominated only judges in favor of human rights. Under this new court, the laws that had limited trials were ruled unconstitutional in 2005. "Kirchner reformed the Supreme Court of Justice, because before it was filled with people from the dictatorial era. So, the issue wasn't simply that justice is slow, but that the judges weren't doing anything," said Juan Carlos (Álvarez, February 2009). Later, President Fernández made speeding up trials against former military officials part of her presidential platform. "The truth is, I strongly support the current Fernández government, and I do so primarily because it was the only one that expressed interest in doing something concrete," said Silvia Martos. "Imagine, more than thirty years pass you by, and only now is there the possibility to actually bring people to trial" (Martos, October 2008). Although there had been a trial against the military leaders in 1985, it was the resumption of trials that led the ex-presos to feel that justice was being served. While Sikkink referred to Argentina's immediate transition period in the 1980s, when constructing her theory on the justice cascade in Latin America, the ex-presos were focused on more recent developments, from 2005 onward.

Third, ex-presos spoke about the Kirchners being good for society in general, that these political leaders were arriving closer to what they envisioned for the country's future. AEPPC member Sebastián Cannizzo (Cannizzo, October 2008) said, "The current government has governed for the country in the interest of the people. . . . It has focused on returning to manufacturing, to jobs, on issues relating to social integration, to housing, and health." Similarly, Juan Carlos said, "Kirchner gave us this economy, of increasing the domestic market, a better distribution of wealth—there's still inequality but he preserved job benefits, improved relations with other Latin American countries" (Álvarez, February 2009). Many ex-presos viewed the Kirchners as developing policy positions that reversed the political agendas of previous administrations and were in line with their own worldviews. One AEPPC member, "Marvin,[1]" however, acknowledged that though the Kirchners were the most important thing to happen to the ex-presos, the current successes were built upon previous initiatives:

> I want to say that the person who is able to do everything today is the Kirchner government, but it wouldn't be fair if we didn't acknowledge that the struggle was started before, like the enormous efforts made by the Madres de Plaza de Mayo. There is no doubt about that. I disagree with others' criticisms of what didn't happen in the past. Kirchner wouldn't have been able to do what he has done without the previous struggles. That the doors were opened because of the struggles, so that later, things could be concretized, because you can only have this fight today because they were always fighting. We didn't see any benefits for a while, or it seemed like nothing came of the struggles, until one day, the world changed and it provided an opportunity. The opportunity came with this government: the ability to hold trials, recover sites like the ESMA and La Perla—it's a question of politics.

The families of the disappeared have done a tremendous of work in advancing human rights, and bravely so. Yet, Marvin's comment explains why ex-presos felt neglected for so many decades; it wasn't until they felt the political climate had changed in their favor that they started to gain recognition as victims. The Kirchners' support for the establishment of memorial museums has provided ex-presos with a space to present themselves as activists to the public. The Kirchners' establishment of human rights offices has also given ex-presos a place to direct their demands for reparations. More than the sum of the actions the Kirchners took—creating memorialized spaces, reopening trials, and establishing government entities in charge of human rights—the real triumph was their ability to establish a normative political environment in favor of human rights.

Of the remaining seventeen ex-presos who did not respond with los Kirchner, sixteen replied, *los juicios,* or "the trials." Ex-presos viewed the trials that have reopened since 2005, and particularly the 2008 trial against General Menéndcz in Córdoba, as significant to their fight for justice. AEPPC member Luís Acosta said, "I think the trials are the most important. Personally I don't think there is any human punishment that is sufficient enough for something like this, but I think it's still good in that it transmits the experience; it passes on our recent history" (Acosta, November 2008). Even with the 1984 truth commission and the 1985 trial, ex-presos believed that the public remained ignorant of the past, and that too few teachers knew enough about recent history to teach younger generations. The trials, then, were a way to educate the masses about the crimes committed against them and their disappeared compañeros. Another AEPPC member, Jorge Alfredo Torriglia, said:

> The government did nothing better than open the trials against the former military officials. This had symbolic significance and it was good for the national psyche because the military's disappearances traumatized every Argentine citizen. This trauma continued with impunity. When the Argentine government made the decision to promote and pressure the judicial branch to try the military, the people began to feel a sense of peace that then allowed them to think about activism. Why? Because the trauma that the military inflicted was an effort to prevent us from organizing our communities, an

attempt to get us to fight among ourselves. . . . Having more pro-
found reflections about activism enables us to organize for more
things, to fight for more justice, equality, for better distribution of
wealth. (Torrigilia, November 2008)

For the ex-presos who viewed the trials as being the most significant
for them, their significance was not limited to putting particular former
military officials behind prison. The trials, instead, were welcomed for
their effects upon society—to better educate others about the past and to
redeem the value of political activism.

The one ex-preso who did not respond with los Kirchner or with los
juicios, said instead, *nada,* or "nothing." AEPPC member Norma Peralta
explained:

What can I say? All of the governments have done nothing. They
haven't done anything, absolutely nothing, except for the indemnity in '91. But the reparation wasn't well conceived, and it created
problems and contradictions for the recipients because everyone
questioned whether to accept it, including the human rights organizations. Here, they don't support the political prisoners. We were
not only victims of state terrorism. It wasn't simply about being
beaten, but that at every corner we were beaten; the whole family
was affected. You had to reinsert yourself in society as an anonymous person. The job situation was precarious. Your own family
doesn't even understand you and blames you for having done something bad. (Peralta, October 2008)

Norma articulates precisely why the ex-presos formed their own organization, and why transitional justice in Argentina had failed to meet their
needs. While reparations could have been seen as the most significant ges-
ture toward victims of state terrorism, they fell short economically and
symbolically. Ex-presos could not wait for the bonds to mature and, for
those who did wait, the economic collapse in 2001, devalued their worth.
Symbolically, the reparations failed because they were given in recognition
not of the fact that survivors were victimized, but rather that they were
inhibited from working. In addition, other human rights groups, by reject-
ing their reparation money, left those who did accept their indemnity

with the feeling that they were making some kind of moral compromise. Norma's comment that the human rights organizations did not support the indemnities is another layer on top of the accusation that ex-presos survived prison by betraying others.

The families of the disappeared rejected reparations in part because they were given during the same time in which Alfonsín pardoned all those who had been sentenced. Thus, when Alfonsín's government awarded 224,000 pesos in bonds to the family of each disappeared person in 1994 (Law 24.411), the move was considered highly controversial and many felt guilty about accepting them (Guembe 2006). One faction of the Madres, the Association of Madres de Plaza de Mayo, denounced the payments as "blood money," and the group's president, Hebe de Bonafini, said that accepting the reparations would amount to the Madres "prostituting themselves" (Ibid., 38). Families were concerned that the reparations were intended to buy their silence, in exchange for the impunity that had already been granted to perpetrators (Ibid., 35). The fact that ex-presos accepted reparations suggests that they lacked integrity; if it was seen as acceptable for ex-presos to take this money, it meant that they were held to a different standard—a lower one.

Norma emphasized that ex-presos continued to suffer after their release from prison. The types of suffering that she identifies are legacies of having been imprisoned and labeled as terrorists-traitors. They returned to estranged family members, they struggled to find employment, and they hid their identities in order to reintegrate into society. The fact that the political prisoners cited los Kirchner as the major success that the government has achieved for the survivors, indicates that transitional justice is an ongoing process. That is, the election of the Kirchners signaled a change in the general context in which various political goals were, or could be, achieved. Trials were one of the transitional justice efforts that exemplified a positive step toward human rights for ex-presos, and those who named trials specifically as the most important state effort were also focused on how the trials impacted the general societal attitudes about the past and toward the victims. If, as Marvin argues, the previous struggles and various transitional justice efforts made immediately after the fall of the dictatorship were important to opening doors three decades later, then a post–transitional justice era should also be seen as equally crucial to the recovery process.

That the ex-presos speak about the legacies of torture and imprisonment as the most impactful on their lives, and that they still seek reparatory measures, suggests that the post–transitional justice period is about
attending to multiple ways in which victims and citizens continue to deal
with the past. Furthermore, a post-transitional period also provides a
space to complicate the black-and-white image of victims and perpetrators that often characterizes initial human rights campaigns to stop gross
human rights violations. The gray areas around victims allow societies to
move away from thinking in absolutes. All those disappeared hadn't done
something wrong to be taken. But some of the disappeared were part of
armed revolutions—did they deserve to be taken? What does it mean for
former armed militants to have their rights taken away and to be subjected to torture? The varying levels of social and economic treatment of
victims, in fact, not only questions how reparations have been or have not
been attentive to the needs of all victims, but also how the narrow concep-
tion of victimhood has denied others a right to symbolic and economic
reparation.

Although this research is a case study based on one group of ex-presos
in Argentina, it has broader implications for other societies undergoing
transitional justice processes. The marginalization of ex-presos and the val-
orization of desaparecidos—two groups of individuals who were compañeros in the same kinds of organizations and movements—demonstrates the
importance of voice. The identities of those who are absent, like the desaparecidos, can be more easily manipulated because they no longer have a
voice to express dissension among them and to contest the simplistic nar-
rations of the past. Families are able to speak about the desaparecidos—a
diverse group of people in fact—as a single, tragic figure. Reducing any
group of victims to an idealized figure falls into the trap of victim versus
perpetrator binaries that do little to teach us about making difficult moral
decisions before genocide occurs, in the period before mass violence. The
dichotomized victim versus perpetrator narrative provides clear targets to
direct blame or innocence but can render invisible, the supporting roles in
government repression, including businesses, neighbors, judges, universities, and indifferent citizens. The silencing of ex-presos was not due merely
to suspicion and condemnation, but was also a result of the impossibility
of easily creating one voice out of many. The political prisoners do not fit

the innocent, apolitical image of victims that generates public sympathy, and by not doing so, they require social and political movements to gather momentum to change how the public thinks in the present about human rights, so that the past can be seen differently.

Another lesson learned from the fact that state violence affects victims over the course of their lives, is that efforts in the immediate transition period can sufficiently redress the grievances of victims. Giving reparations once is not enough for survivors who continue to face problems in the post-dictatorship era. Transitional justice processes are often nonlinear and involve setbacks, adjustments, and minor successes. But just as the damage done to survivors endures over time, transitional justice policies should be conceived as an ongoing political commitment.

The way in which ex-presos are aging is one illustration of why transitional justice is a long-term process. Aging is not only about the decline of physical and mental health, but also about previous life events positively or negatively affecting one's later status in life. Rather than arguing that the types of abuses the ex-presos suffered are too difficult to measure and to compensate, instead it is incumbent upon political leaders, scholars, and citizens to conceptualize a post-transitional justice process that addresses the legacies of state terrorism. Undoubtedly, recovery processes in post-conflict situations take time, and they are beholden to the general societal context and depend upon the government's ability to enact reparatory measures. The current organizing efforts of the AEPPC three decades after the fall of the dictatorship, however, demonstrate just how long the effects of state terrorism last, and correspondingly, how long the process of transitional justice must continue. In Argentina and elsewhere, we have found ourselves still facing an era of post-transitional justice.

Epilogue

Several dramatic changes happened to the AEPPC since I left Argentina in 2009. During the years I observed the ex-presos, the AEPPC met on a regular basis, and the forty-five members who regularly attended, were in agreement over the group's agenda and generally enjoyed a strong sense of camaraderie. The AEPPC formed officially in 2007; as stated in its bylaws, it was required to hold elections every two years for the positions of president, vice president, treasurer, and secretary. When elections were held in 2009, tensions arose, but the ex-presos continued to work together, and in 2011, they became the first group of political prisoners to establish an office in Córdoba and to receive a government subsidy to cover operating costs. On October 1, 2011, when the AEPPC held elections again, two separate lists of candidates were proposed. The candidates who lost the elections stopped attending AEPPC meetings, but continued to operate under the AEPPC name. Since then, there have been several internal disagreements, most significantly, over the passage of a provincial reparation law in Córdoba.

When the Córdoba provincial government passed a law awarding pensions to former political prisoners on March 24, 2012, many AEPPC members were shocked to learn that the version of the law passed was not the one that had been agreed upon earlier. It turned out that two AEPPC members had privately met with the lawmakers and made a deal that was not in accordance with what the general membership of the AEPPC demanded.

Provincial legislator, Carlos Alessandri, introduced a pension law for political prisoners on March 12, 2012, and it was later passed on March 24, 2012, the National Day of Memory for Truth and Justice. This law awards a monthly pension that amounts to 3,000 pesos, which is double the minimum retirement pension in Córdoba Province, and is worth approximately $685 in U.S. dollars. These pensions, on the one hand, publicly acknowledge and compensate the suffering experienced by political prisoners, but they have, on the other hand, divided the political prisoner community—legitimizing some and not others.

The controversy over this law is due to the requirements to qualify for this pension. Among other conditions, beneficiaries had to have been imprisoned for political reasons for more than a year between March 24, 1976, and December 10, 1983, and they must have been detained in Córdoba Province. While there are other requirements that the human rights community opposes (e.g., recipients must have lived in Córdoba for at least ten years), these conditions do not reflect how political prisoners actually experienced state terrorism. In fact, this research demonstrates the problems with all three of these conditions.

First, the length of time spent in prison did not necessarily determine post-release experiences. Even those who were detained for several months or even a week, suffered torture—the impacts of simulated executions, waterboarding, and electrocution are horrifying and enduring even when torture acts happen only once—and they also experienced social and economic discrimination after being marked by the military as "subversive." The long-term impacts of torture are still not widely understood, but AEPPC members believe it has shortened their life expectancies. The social stigma attached to imprisonment—however brief—meant that people were no longer willing to associate with political prisoners, cutting off their job and social opportunities.

Counting the time spent in prison between the official start and end dates of the dictatorship, overlooks how the repression actually began, and when the concentration camps were piloted. Like other cases of mass violence, the disappearances and systematic torture of victims did not suddenly begin once the military took power on March 24, 1976; instead, right-wing forces had already been killing, torturing, and imprisoning political dissidents for some time. When the military took power, they simply expanded the number of disappearances and created more secret detention centers. It is for this reason that so many of the political prisoners interviewed here were detained in 1974 and 1975, before the start of the military dictatorship.

The new pension law also fails to correspond to how the system of disappearances and imprisonment actually operated. Political prisoners were transferred to several clandestine detention centers and therefore often spent time in more than one province. In some cases, political prisoners were detained in other provinces and kept in other prisons before being later transferred to Córdoba.

For former AEPPC president Sara Liliana Waitman, that the AEPPC has been able to work in solidarity with other groups around pensions has been the most successful part of the process (personal correspondence, March 12, 2012). The pension law, while imperfect, is a step in the right direction. With this as the basis of economic reparations, political prisoners can continue to lobby the government to expand its coverage.

In a public statement explaining why they reject Córdoba's pension law, the National Association of Political Prisoners wrote, "We do not accept this policy that serves to divide us, that forces us to break our common cause that unites us nationally and that seeks to distract us by forcing us to divide our energies on a province by province basis" (April 2, 2012). In addition, this association also rejects the pension laws passed in Misiones and Mendoza, which provide a small stipend (900 and 1,900 pesos, respectively) to a select group of people who meet the eligibility requirements, and instead upholds the pension law passed by Buenos Aires Province (Law 14042), which provides 3,680 pesos on a monthly basis, distributed to all political prisoners without any distinctions.

The association continued to lobby for a national pension law for all former political prisoners. After four years of campaigning for reparations, as this book went to press, the political prisoners finally won a second set of reparations. On November 28, 2013, Congress passed a law granting monthly pensions of approximately 5,000 to 6,000 pesos to former political prisoners or their inheritors. What made this law remarkable, was that it recognized all those imprisoned before December 10, 1983, and thereby expanded the number of potential recipients beyond those who were imprisoned only between 1976 and 1983. Meanwhile, some of the AEPPC members have left the organization and founded *Ex Presos Políticos por la Patria Grande* (Former Political Prisoners for the Greater Fatherland) in September 2013. Both organizations continue to work in Córdoba.

NOTES

CHAPTER 1: "THE BATTLE OF THE PANTIES"

1. The Spanish word *desaparecer* (to disappear) became a part of the new vocabulary of life under state repression. As a transitive verb, "to disappear someone," meant that the military kidnapped and tortured victims in secret torture camps; but there are no legal records. After the military killed "disappeared persons," they disposed of the bodies in unmarked graves or at the bottom of the Atlantic Ocean to intentionally eliminate evidence. Just as the Spanish language reflected this reality, I adopt the same usage in English.
2. In Spanish, the word used was *chupar.*
3. Argentine human rights activists speak about their activism as demands for memory, truth, and justice, and often refer to the immediate post-dictatorship era as the time in which their country "returned to democracy."
4. During the dictatorship, the military dispatched groups of men dressed in civilian clothing whose objective was to hunt down their targets through surveillance and large-scale operations. These men were armed and worked with both the military and the police to kidnap and to disappear people with collaboration from nearly all levels of authority, including the justice system.
5. There existed other human rights organizations before, during, and after the dictatorship, including the Argentine League for the Rights of Man, the Ecumenical Movement for Human Rights, and the Peace and Justice Service. The family-based groups, however, became the dominant actors in Argentina's transitional justice process. I discuss the formation of the AEPPC in relation only to the family-based groups, because they are the major figures in the Argentine human rights movement.
6. In Córdoba, there were two D2 locations. One was located on Mariano Moreno, and the other was located next door to the town's cathedral, in one part of the Cabildo.
7. While the former political prisoners did not recognize any specific patterns in where they were taken, I noticed that prisoners in Córdoba after 1976, were often taken to D2, then to La Perla and to La Ribera, and eventually to UP1. At UP1, the men and women were separated and transferred to another concentration camp, or to the large prison Villa Devoto in Buenos Aires if they were women, and Penitentiary Unit Number 9 in La Plata (U9) if they

were men. While torture was the most severe in the beginning, and prisoners were tortured throughout their detainment at various places, Villa Devoto and U9 were "legal" prisons that allowed prisoners to have more interaction and restricted privileges. However, prisoners at Villa Devoto and at U9 were still subjected to various forms of torture and humiliating procedures designed to demoralize them. Prison guards purposely tried to prevent prisoners from forming relationships in prison. These two prisons were frequently the last places in the network prisoners went to before they were ultimately released.

8. The term *compañero* approximates the words "comrade," "colleague," and "partner." AEPPC members use the term to mean "fellow activist," unless speaking about those they are in a relationship with, in which case it means "boyfriend" or "girlfriend" or "spouse." In Argentina specifically, the term carries a shared political commitment that comes out of the Peronist movement, but is also shared widely across the Marxist, Trotskyite, and other revolutionary groups. In Spanish, the term is also specified in terms of gender as compañero for men, and compañera for women.

9. *Carmelo* or "hard candy" was the slang word for the secret messages wrapped up in bits of plastic that prisoners wrote and carried to others by holding them in their mouths, or by swallowing and later defecating them. Guards often subjected prisoners to invasive bodily inspections, looking for small objects and messages that women hid in their vaginas, and that both men and women carried in their anuses.

10. I left Argentina before this film was completed. Some of the scenes that I screened involved groups of former political prisoners collectively narrating stories about their imprisonment at UP1. One person would begin telling the story, and other participants would join in on the narration, and carry the storyline through until it was finished. One person would speak at a time, but all of the stories had multiple tellers.

11. I acknowledge that there is a massive literature on agency in the social sciences and multiple definitions. For my purposes, I am interested in the concept inasmuch as it allows me to discuss how political prisoners think and speak about their activism. Their desire to resist and to express solidarity is what I consider to be acts of agency. Beyond that, I leave discussions on agency to other scholars who are far more adept on this subject.

12. Her experience was told in the book, *That Inferno* (2006).

CHAPTER 2: "THEY DISOWNED US TWICE"

1. In 1986, the Madres split into two factions. The Madres–Founding Line focuses on finding their disappeared children's remains, and the Association–Madres is more radical in their attempt to change the political system and to support a Cuban Revolution–style movement in Argentina. The former group is more involved in memorialization projects than the latter, which instead supports housing projects and other initiatives to curb social inequalities.

2. For a detailed account of the court proceedings, see Carlos Santiago Niño's (1996) *Radical Evil on Trial.*

3. Ex-preso/a is a gendered pair in Spanish.

4. The white handkerchiefs symbolized their children's diapers; the Madres wore these during their protest marches every Thursday as they walked their rounds in the Plaza de Mayo.

5. President Cristina Fernández de Kirchner appointed Dr. Martín Fresnada as Argentina's new secretary of human rights in May 2012, after the sudden death of Dr. Eduardo Luis Duhalde.

6. *Chocho* refers to the state of being when an outburst of several minor details ends up producing a lot of drama.

CHAPTER 3: SUSPICION AND COLLABORATION

1. I use a pseudonym here because his comments are controversial.

2. The same *Página/12* article also announced that on April 30, 2008, part of the ESMA compound—the naval social club area—would be transformed into a Cultural Center of Our Children and run by the Asociación Madres de Plaza de Mayo. Thus, a compromise had been made to incorporate various kinds of spaces into the ESMA site.

3. I returned to visit the ESMA again in May 2008, with the AEPPC. By that time, quotes from survivors about their time in the attic had been mounted throughout the cells.

CHAPTER 4: SOLIDARITY AND RESISTANCE IN PRISON

1. Cynthia is a pseudonym for one of the political prisoners who spoke about the taboo topic of rape during imprisonment. As Barbara Reinhold noted in "Presas Políticas" in *Clarín*, on May 3, 2012, many women political prisoners were raped in torture camps during the dictatorship.

2. Before La Perla was converted into a concentration camp, it served as a military training ground, and there was a large trough that horses used to drink out of near the old stables. During the dictatorship, that trough was used for the submarine, a method of torture. This water was so putrid that some survivors remember Menéndez ordering subordinates to add perfume to the water before he arrived to mask the smell. The water itself, however, was never changed.

3. Norma purposely avoided using her partner's real name during the interview. Therefore, I avoided using her partner's real name in the text as well.

4. "Charlie" Moore had been an activist in the ERP before he was detained in November 1974, and he remained a prisoner until 1980. During his time as a prisoner, he collaborated with his captors. Upon his release, he lived in exile in London.

5. Chicha is the only member of the AEPPC who was never imprisoned; her inclusion in the organization is based on her solidarity with former political prisoners, in particular, around health issues.

6. That child was the first missing grandchild to be found in Córdoba.
7. Pamela is not in the AEPPC, though she too, is a survivor of the concentration camps and prisons. She was detained for searching for her disappeared brother. While the AEPPC members want their real names used, this woman intentionally avoided being part of the AEPPC, and a result, I chose to use a pseudonym. Fieldnotes, 9/18/2008.
8. *Negro*, literally "black," is often used to describe someone with dark skin or hair.

CHAPTER 5: LIFE AFTER PRISON

1. Although they technically moved out of Argentina, Alicia still considers her time in exile as internal because the majority of her clandestine life took place in her own country, and the physical proximity of, and cultural similarities between, Uruguay and Argentina, did not lead her to perceive her situation as the same as that of those who moved to the United States or to Europe.
2. La Perla was a military training site, and the military transformed the former horse stables into a holding pen for the prisoners.
3. *Biodanza* means "dance of life," and involves music, movement, and interactions whereby participants explore their identities and emotions. It began in Chile in 1970, as a form of psychological therapy.
4. These data are from an interview with Sara Liliana Waitman, and an internal document (4/25/2011) that Sara circulated to the AEPPC. Inspired by my inquiries and comments about a number of recent deaths, Sara decided to begin compiling a list of all ex-presos who died after their release. Included alongside each ex-preso's name is their age at the time of death, and the cause of death, if known. The list is still under construction, and the number—sixty-five—was current as of this writing.
5. I use a pseudonym here because he is speaking about a sensitive matter.

CHAPTER 6: POST-TRANSITIONAL JUSTICE

1. I use a pseudonym here because personal finances can be a sensitive matter.

GLOSSARY

Abuelas Abuelas de Plaza de Mayo (Grandmothers of Plaza de Mayo) are a group of grandmothers who are searching for their missing grandchildren who were stolen and given away to military families and to their supporters under false adoption papers. The military kidnapped approximately 500 babies. By 2013, the Abuelas had recovered the identity of 109 stolen children.

Archivo Comisión y el Archivo Provincial de la Memoria de Córdoba (Provincial Commission and Archive of Memory of Córdoba) currently operates as a memorial museum on military repression, and is housed in the place that once operated as the center of police intelligence from the 1970s, through the last military dictatorship (1976–1983).

AEDD Asociación de Ex Detenidos Desaparecidos (Association of Ex-Detainees and Disappeared) was formed in 1992, in Buenos Aires.

AEPPC Asociación de Ex-Presos Políticos de Córdoba (Association of Former Political Prisoners of Córdoba) formed in 2007, and became the first group of former political prisoners to gain legal status.

CELS Centro de Estudios Legales y Sociales (Center of Legal and Social Studies) is an important human rights group located in Buenos Aires.

CCDs Campos Clandestinos de Detención (Clandestine Detention Centers) was where disappeared victims were tortured and killed.

Compañero The term that political prisoners use to describe their "comrades" in revolutionary movements, but is also used to refer to their work colleagues and romantic partners.

CONADEP Comisión Nacional Sobre la Desaparición de Personas (Argentine National Commission on the Disappeared) was Argentina's truth commission that formed in 1983, and published its report, *Nunca Más*, in 1984.

D2 The former Departamento de Informaciónes de la Policía de la Provincia de Córdoba (Center for Police Intelligence for the Province of Córdoba) was also used as a secret clandestine center to torture and to interrogate disappeared victims during the last military dictatorship (1976–1983), and was also used as a torture center before 1976. It is currently a memorialized site and is the location of the Provincial Commission and Archive for Memory in Córdoba.

ERP Ejército Revolucionario del Pueblo (People's Revolutionary Army) was one of the main guerrilla groups of armed revolutionaries. It was the radical arm of the Revolutionary Worker's Party (PRT).

Eslabones Eslabones: Crónicas, Relatos, Poesías, Cuentos, Ilustraciónes (Links: Chronicles, stories, poetry, tales, and pictures) is the AEPPC's 2009 self-published volume of testimonies.

ESMA Escuela de Mecánica de la Armada (Navy Mechanics School), which operated as a CCD throughout the entire military dictatorship (1976–1983) is the standard against which all other CCDs are measured because of its brutal torture tactics and low survival rates. In 2004, the Argentine government established the ESMA as a memorial museum and renamed it the Espacio para la Memoria y para la Promoción y Defensa de los Derechos Humanos (Space for Memory and for the Promotion and Defense of Human Rights).

Ex-presos The shorthand term for ex–presos políticos, or former political prisoners.

Familiares Familiares de Desaparecidos y Detenidos por Razones Políticas (Families of The Disappeared and Imprisoned for Political Reasons), which formed in 1976, before the Madres de Plaza de Mayo includes siblings, spouses, parents, and other relatives of the desaparecidos. It was initially started by a group of family members in Córdoba and was called the Comisión de Familiares de Detenidos Políticos (Commission of Families of Political Detainees).

HIJOS Hijos e Hijas por la Identidad y la Justicia contra el Olvido y el Silencio (Children for Identity and Justice and against Forgetting and Silence), formed in Córdoba and in La Plata in 1995, during Menem's presidency, which was known as the era of impunity. They are known for their protests outside of the homes of known former military officials who were responsible for the deaths of disappeared victims.

Madres Madres de Plaza de Mayo (Mothers of Plaza de Mayo) were the first to openly protest the dictatorship in 1977. The organization split into two divisions in 1986: Madres Línea Fundadora (Mothers Founding Line), and Asociación de Madres de Plaza de Mayo (Association of Mothers of Plaza de Mayo).

Mílico Derogatory slang to refer to the military.

Montoneros The leftist armed branch of the Peronist Party.

PC Partido Comunista (Communist Party).

PEN Poder Ejecutivo Nacional (National Executive Authority) was where some political prisoners were arrested and held under PEN.

La Perla One of the largest CCDs in Argentina, located in Córdoba Province, was where victims were tortured and kept before being killed or transferred to another CCD. Approximately 2,200 victims were killed at La Perla.

El Proceso Proceso de Reoganización Nacional (Process for National Reorganization) was the term used by the military dictatorship to justify taking over the country.

PRT Partido Revolucionario de los Trabajadores (Workers' Revolutionary Party) was a Marxist-Leninist political organization in Argentina.

La Ribera A concentration camp in Córdoba that was used as a secret detention center.

Triple A Alianza Anticomunista Argentina (Argentine Anti-Communist Alliance).

U9 Unidad 9 de La Plata (Penitentiary Unit Number 9 of La Plata), was one of the regular prisons where male political prisoners were held during the military dictatorship.

UP1 Unidad Penitenciaria 1 de San Martín (Penitentiary Unit Number 1 of San Martín) in Córdoba, was one of the regular prisons where both male and female political prisoners were held in separate pavilions during the military dictatorship.

Villa Devoto A prison in Buenos Aires Province that held female political prisoners during the military dictatorship.

REFERENCES

Abregú, Martín. 2000. "Human Rights after the Dictatorship: Lessons from Argentina." *NACLA Report of the Americas* 34 (1): 12–18.

Actis, Munú, Cristina Aldini, Liliana Gardella, Miriam Lewin, and Elisa Tokar. 2006. *That Inferno.* Translated by Gretta Siebentritt. Nashville: Vanderbilt University Press.

Acuña, Carlos H., and Catalina Smulovitz. 1995. "Militares en la transición argentina: Del gobierno a la subordinación constitucional [Soldiers in the Argentine transition: From government to constitutional subordination]." In *Juicio, castigo y memorias: Derechos humanos y justicia en la política argentina* [Justice, punishment, and memories: Human rights and justice in Argentine politics]. Edited by Carlos H. Acuña, 21–99. Buenos Aires: Ediciones Nueva Visión.

Ageitos, Stella Maris. 2002. *Historia de la impunidad: De los actas de Videla a los indultos de Menem* [History of impunity: From the minutes of Videla to the pardons of Menem]. Buenos Aires: Adriana Hidalgo.

Amnesty International. 1979. *Testimonio sobre campos secretos de detención en Argentina.* Nottingham, England: Russell Press.

Arditti, Rita. 1999. *Searching for Life: The Grandmothers of the Plaza de Mayo and the Disappeared Children of Argentina.* Berkeley: University of California Press.

Arthur, Paige. 2009. "How 'Transitions' Reshaped Human Rights: A Conceptual History of Transitional Justice." *Human Rights Quarterly* 30: 321–367.

Asociación Civil El Periscopio. 2003. *Del otro lado de la mirilla: Olvidos y memorias de expresos políticos de Coronda 1974–1979* [From the other side of the peephole: Forgettings and memories of former political prisoners of Coronda 1974–1979]. Santa Fe: El Periscopio.

Asociación de Ex Presos Políticos de Córdoba. 2009. *Eslabones* [Links]. Córdoba: Asociación de Ex Presos Políticos de Córdoba.

Bejarano, Cynthia. 2002. Las Super Madres de Latino America: Transforming Motherhood by Challenging Violence in Mexico, Argentina, and El Salvador. *Frontiers: Journal of Women Studies* 23(1):126–150.

Berguan, Viviana, ed. 2006. *Nosotras, presas políticas: Obra colectiva de 112 prisionerapolíticas entre 1974 y 1983* [We, political prisoners: Collective work of 112 female political prisoners between 1974 and 1983]. Buenos Aires: Nuestra America.

Betrisey, Débora. 2012. "Inmigración, política y protesta popular contra la explotación laboral en Buenos Aires, Argentina [Immigration, politics, and popular protest against labor exploitation in Buenos Aires, Argentina]." *Journal of Latin American and Caribbean Anthropology* 17 (2): 279–298.

Bonaldi, Pablo. 2003. "Hijos de desaparecidos: Entre la construcción de la política y la construcción de la memoria [Children of the disappeared: Between the construction of politics and the construction of memory]." In *Programa de formación e investigación sobre memoria colectiva y represión: Perspectivas comparativas sobre el proceso de democratización en el Cono Sur y el Perú-SSRC* [Program of training and research on collective memory and repression: Comparative perspectives on the process of democratization in the Southern Cone and Peru, Social Science Research Council]. Unpublished paper.

Bonasso, Miguel. 1984. *Recuerdo de la muerte* [Memory of death]. Buenos Aires: Puntosur.

Borer, Tristan Anne. 2003. "A Taxonomy of Victims and Perpetrators: Human Rights and Reconciliation in South Africa." *Human Rights Quarterly* 25 (4): 1088–1116.

Bosco, Fernando J. 2008. "Place, Space, Networks, and the Sustainability of Collective Action: The Madres de Plaza de Mayo." *Global Networks* 1(4):307–329.

Bouvard, Marguerite Guzmán. 1994. *Revolutionizing Motherhood: The Mothers of Plaza de Mayo*. Lanham, MD: Rowman & Littlefield.

Brysk, Alison. 1994. *The Politics of Human Rights in Argentina*. Stanford, CA: Stanford University Press.

Calviero, Pilar. 1998. *Poder y desaparición* [Power and disappearance]. Buenos Aires: Colihue.

CONADEP. 1986 [1984]. *Nunca más: Informe de la Comisión Nacional Sobre la Desaparición de Personas.* [Never again: The Report of the Argentine National Commission on the Disappeared]. London: Faber & Faber.

Daleo, Graciela. 1998. "Testimonio de los ex detenidos-desaparecidos [Testimony of the ex–detained and disappeared]." In *Contra la impunidad: Simposio contra la impunidad y en defense de los derechos humanos* [Against impunity: Symposium against impunity and in defense of human rights]. Edited by Plataforma Argentina contra la impunidad Barcelona, 237–241. Barcelona: Icaria Editorial.

Damonte, Jorge Luis. 2013. "Los Efectos en la Salud en Sobrevivientes del Terrorismo de Estado." [The effects of state terrorism on survivors]. *El Mortero.* Accessed August 1, 2013, http://www.elmorterodigital.com.ar/node/163.

Da Silva Catela, Ludmila. 2001. *No habrá flores en la tumba del pasado: La experiencia de reconstrucción del mundo de los familiares de desaparecidos* [There will not be flowers on the tomb of the past: The experience of the reconstruction of the world of the families of the disappeared]. La Plata: Ediciones Al Margen.

Das, Veena. 2006. *Life and Words: Violence and the Descent into the Ordinary.* Berkeley: University of California Press.

David, Roman, and Susanne Choi Yuk-ping. 2005. "Victims on Transitional Justice: Lessons from the Reparation of Human Rights Abuses in the Czech Republic." *Human Rights Quarterly* 27(2): 392–435.

Diez, Rolo. 2000. *Los compañeros* [The compañeros]. La Plata: Ed. de la Campana.

Dinerstein, Ana. 2002. "The Battle of Buenos Aires: Crisis, Insurrection and the Reinvention of Politics in Argentina." *Historical Materialism* 10 (4): 5–38.

Familiares de Desaparecidos y Detenidos por Razones Políticas de Córdoba. 2006. *La teoría de los dos demonios: Una falsa justificación del terrorismo de estado* [The two demons theory: A false justification of state terrorism]. Archival Document, 7. Córdoba, Argentina, Familiares.

Faulk, Karen Ann. 2012. *In the Wake of Neoliberalism: Citizenship and Human Rights in Argentina.* Stanford: Stanford University Press.

Feitlowitz, Marguerite. 1998. *A Lexicon of Terror: Argentina and the Legacies of Torture.* Oxford: Oxford University Press.

Feld, Claudia. 2002. *Del estrado a la pantalla: Las imagines del juicio a los ex comandantes en Argentina* [From the stage to the screen: Images of the trial of former commanders in Argentina]. Madrid, Buenos Aires: Siglo XXI.

Frankl, Viktor E. 1985[1946]. *Man's Search for Meaning.* New York: Washington Square Press.

Garay, Candelaria. 2007. "Social Policy and Collective Action: Unemployed Workers, Community Associations, and Protest in Argentina." *Politics & Society* 35 (2): 301–328.

Gelman, Juan, and Mara La Madrid. 1997. *Ni el flaco perdón de Dios: Hijos de desaprecidos* [God forgives not even the skinny one]. Buenos Aires: Planeta.

Gobierno de la Provincia de Córdoba, 2009. Secretaría de Derechos Humanos. *Census de ex–presos políticos en Córdoba* [Census of former political prisoners in Córdoba]. Córdoba: Secretaría de Derechos Humanos de la Provincia de Córdoba.

Grandin, Greg. 2005. "The Instruction of Great Catastrophe: Truth Commission, National History, and State Formation in Argentina, Chile, and Guatemala." *American Historical Review* 110 (1): 46–67.

Guelar, Diana, Vera Jarach, and Beatriz Ruiz. 2002. *Los chicos del exilio: Argentina (1975—1984)* [The youths of exile: Argentina 1975–1984]. Buenos Aires: Ediciones del País Nomeolvides.

Guembe, Maria José. 2006. "Economic Reparations for Grave Human Rights Violations: The Argentinean Experience." In *The Handbook of Reparations.* Edited by Pablo De Grieff, 21–44. Oxford: Oxford University Press.

Guest, Iain. 1990. *Behind the Disappearances: Argentina's Dirty War against Human Rights and the United Nations.* Philadelphia: University of Pennsylvania Press.

Heker, Liliana. 1996. *El fin de la historia* [The end of the story]. Buenos Aires: Alfaguara.

Humphrey, Michael, and Estela Valverde. 2008. "Human Rights Politics and Injustice: Transitional Justice in Argentina and South Africa." *International Journal of Transitional Justice* 2: 83–105.

Inter-American Commission on Human Rights. 1980. *Report on the Situation of Human Rights in Argentina.* Washington, DC: General Secretariat Organization of American States.

Jelin, Elizabeth. 2009. "Victims, Relatives, and Citizens in Argentina: Whose Voice Is Legitimate Enough?" In *Humanitarianism and Suffering: The Mobilization of*

Empathy. Edited by Richard Ashby Wilson and Richard D. Brown, 177–201. Cambridge: Cambridge University Press.

Jelin, Elizabeth, and Susana G. Kaufman. 2000. "Layers of Memories: Twenty Years After in Argentina." In *The Politics of War, Memory and Commemoration*. Edited by T. G. Ashplant, Graham Dawson, and Michael Roper, 89–110. London: Routledge.

Keck, Margaret C., and Kathryn Sikkink. 1998. *Activists beyond Borders: Advocacy Networks in International Politics*. Ithaca: Cornell University Press.

Keys, Barbara. 2012. "Anti-Torture Politics: Amnesty International, the Greek Junta, and the Origins of the Human Rights 'Boom' in the United States." In *The Human Rights Revolution: An International History*. Edited by Akira Iriye, Petra Goedde, and William I. Hitchcock, 201–221. Oxford: Oxford University Press.

Laplante, Lisa J. 2008. "Transitional Justice and Peace Building: Diagnosing and Addressing the Socioeconomic Roots of Violence through a Human Rights Framework." *International Journal of Transitional Justice* 2 (3): 331–355.

Leebaw, Bronwyn Anne. 2008. "The Irreconcilable Goals of Transitional Justice." *Human Rights Quarterly* 30: 95–118.

Levi, Primo. 1989 [1986]. *The Drowned and the Saved*. Translated by Raymond Rosenthal. New York: Vintage International.

Longoni, Ana. 2007. *Traiciones: La figura del traidor en los relatos acerca de los sobrevivientes de la represión* [Treacheries: The figure of the traitor in stories about the survivors of the repression]. Buenos Aires: Grupo Editorial Norma.

Lorenz, Federico G. 2002. "¿De quién es el 24 de marzo? Las luchas por la memoria delgolpe de 1976 [Whose is March 24th? The fights for the memory of the coup of 1976]." In *Las conmemoraciones: Las disputas en las fechas "in-felices"* [Commemorations: The disputes about the "unlucky" dates]. Edited by Elizabeth Jelin, 53–100. Madrid, Buenos Aires: Siglo XXI.

Marchak, Patricia. 1999. *God's Assassins: State Terrorism in Argentina in the 1970s*. Montreal: McGill-Queen's University Press.

McKinney, Kelly. 2007. "Breaking the Conspiracy of Silence: Testimony, Traumatic Memory, and Psychotherapy with Survivors of Political Violence" *Ethos* 35 (3): 265–299.

Merenson, Silvina, and Santiago Garaño. 2010. Introduction to "Dossier: La prisión política en al Argentina, entre la historia y la memoria (1966–1983) [Dossier: The political prison in Argentina, between history and memory]." In *Ibero Americana* 40: 87–92.

Miller, Zinaida. 2008. "Effects of Invisibility: In Search of the 'Economic' in Transitional Justice." *International Journal of Transitional Justice* 2: 266–291.

Moyn, Samuel. 2010. *The Last Utopia*. Cambridge: Belknap Press of Harvard University Press.

Muvingi, Ismael. 2009. "Sitting on Powder Kegs: Socioeconomic Rights in Transitional Societies." *International Journal of Transitional Justice* 3: 163–182.

Niño, Carlos Santiago. 1996. *Radical Evil on Trial*. New Haven: Yale University Press.

Novarro, Marcos, and Vicente Palermo. 2003. *La dictadura militar (1976–1983): Del golpe de estado a la democracia* [The military dictatorship (1976–1983): From coup d'état to democracy]. Buenos Aires: Paidós.

Oberti, Alejandra, and Roberto Pittaluga. 2006. *Memorias en montaje. Escrituras de la militancia y pensamientos sobre la historia* [Memories in montage: Writings from the militancy and thoughts on history]. Buenos Aires: Ediciones El Cielo por Asalto.

Partnoy, Alicia. 1986. *La escuelita: Relatos testimoniales* [The little school: Testimonial stories]. Buenos Aires: Editorial La Bohemia.

Payne, Leigh. 2003. "Perpetrators' Confessions: Truth, Reconciliation, and Justice in Argentina." In *What Justice? Whose Justice? Fighting for Fairness in Latin America.* Edited by Susan E. Eckstein and Timothy P. Wickham-Crowley, 158–184. Berkeley: University of California Press.

Perelli, Carina. 1994. "Memoria de Sangre: Fear, Hope and Disenchantment in Argentina." In *Remapping Memory: The Politics of Time and Space.* Edited by Jonathan Boyarin, 39–66. Minneapolis: University of Minnesota Press.

Reinhold, Barbara. 2012. "Presas Políticas." *Clarín.* May 3, accessed December 1, 2013, http://www.clarin.com/sociedad/Presas-politicas_0_658134349.html.

Robben, Antonius C.G.M. 2005. *Political Violence and Trauma in Argentina.* Philadelphia: University of Pennsylvania Press.

Robins, Simon. 2011. "Towards Victim-Centred Transitional Justice: Understanding the Needs of Families of the Disappeared in Postconflict Nepal." *Human Rights Quarterly* 5: 75–98.

Roman, David, and Susanne Choi Yuk-Ping. 2005. "Victims on Transitional Justice: Lessons from the Reparation of Human Rights Abuses in the Czech Republic." *Human Rights Quarterly* 27: 392–435.

Romero, Simon, and Jonathan Gilbert. 2013. "Argentina Finds a Dictatorship's Secret Records." *New York Times.* November 5, accessed January 1, 2014, http://www.nytimes.com/2013/11/06/world/americas/argentina-finds-a-dictatorships-secret-records.html?_r=0.

de Saint-Exupéry, Antoine. 1995 [1943]. *The Little Prince.* Translated by Irene Testot-Ferry. Ware, Hertfordshire: Wordsworth Classics.

Skaar, Elin. 2011. *Judicial Independence and Human Rights in Latin America: Violations, Politics, and Prosecution.* New York: Palgrave Macmillan.

Sillato, Maria del Carmen, ed. 2008. *Huellas: Memorias de Resistencia (Argentina 1974–1983)* [Footprints: Memories of resistance (Argentina 1974–1983)]. San Luis: Nueva Editorial Universitaria.

Sikkink, Kathryn. 2011. *The Justice Cascade: How Human Rights Prosecutions Are Changing World Politics.* New York: W. W. Norton.

Stover, Eric, and Elena O. Nightingale, eds. 1985. *The Breaking of Bodies and Minds: Torture, Psychiatric Abuse, and the Health Professions.* New York: W. H. Freeman.

Suárez- Orozco, Marcelo. 2004. "The Treatment of Children in the 'Dirty War': Ideology, State Terrorism, and the Abuse of Children in Argentina." In *Violence in*

War and Peace. Edited by Nancy Scheper-Hughes and Philippe Bourgois, 378-388. Oxford: Blackwell.

Taylor, Julie. 2001. "Desdemona's Lament." *Drama Review* 45 (4): 106–124.

Timerman, Jacobo. 1998[1981]. *Prisoner Without a Name, Cell Without a Number*. Translated by Toby Talbot. New York: Vintage Books.

Todorov, Tzvetan. 1996 [1991]. *Facing the Extreme: Moral Life in the Concentration Camps*. New York: Henry Holt.

Van Drunen, Saskia. 2010. *Struggling with the Past: The Human Rights Movements and the Politics of Memory in Post-Dictatorship Argentina (1983–2006)*. Amsterdam: Rozenberg Publishers.

Vezzetti, Hugo. 2002. *Pasado y presente: Guerra, dictadura y sociedad en la Argentina* [Past and present: War, dictatorship, and society in Argentina]. Buenos Aires and Madrid: Siglo XXI.

Weschler, Lawrence. 1990. *A Miracle, A Universe: Settling Accounts with Torturers*. Chicago and London: University of Chicago Press.

Williams, Paul. 2007. *Memorial Museums: The Global Rush to Commemorate Atrocities*. Oxford: Berg.

LIST OF FORMER POLITICAL PRISONERS

Luís Acosta, November 14, 2008
Fidel Antonio Alcázar, October 21, 2008
Juan Carlos Álvarez, February 25, 2009
Hugo Argente, February 14, 2008
Américo Aspitia, April 22, 2009
Atilio Basso, October 23, 2008
Maria Mercedes "Chicha" Aranguren e Scheurer, September 18, 2008
Jorge L. "Caballo" Argañaraz, September 1, 2008
Ester Cabral, November 2, 2008
Sebastián Cannizzo, October 22, 2008
Irma Casas, August 15, 2008
Ludmila da Silva Catela, June 3, 2009
Miguel Carlos "Miguelito" Contreras, September 22, 2008
Félix "Gato" Cornejo, August 20, 2008
Cristina Correa, September 11, 2008
María Cristina Díaz, December 4, 2008
Graciela Josefina Felisa Donato de Suárez, August 13, 2008
D2 guided tour, Córdoba June 8, 2008
Élida "Ely" Eichenberger, October 28, 2008
ESMA guided tour, Buenos Aires, February 18, 2008
Hugo "Siete" Fernández, December 10, 2008
Hugo "Gato" Ferrandans, May 9, 2009
Víctor Eduardo Ferraro, April 20, 2009
Ovidio Ramón "Pajarito" Ferreyra, October 27, 2008
Pedro Gaetán, November 9, 2008
Silvia Martos, October 29, 2008
Manuel Nieva, September 5, 2008
Rosa Noto, September 18, 2008
Rodolfo "Petiso" Novillo, September 23, 2008
"Pamela", September 18, 2008
Norma Peralta, October 30, 2008
María del Carmen "Carmencita" Pérez, August 24, 2008

Jorge "Villero" Ramírez, November 28, 2008
Gladys Regalado, September 3, 2008
Enzo "Gringo" Sacco, September 19, 2008
Alicia Staps, November 6, 2008
Carlos Hugo Suárez, August 13, 2008
Jorge Alfredo Torriglia, November 17, 2008
Adriana Varillas, December 12, 2008
Alicia Varillas, December 12, 2008
Viviana "Vivi" Vergara, August 25, 2008
Juan Villa, May 21, 2009
Sara Liliana Waitman, August 28 and September 4, 2008
Heldo Zárate, November 4, 2008

INDEX

Abuelas de la Plaza de Mayo, 2, 11, 29, 31, 34, 37, 41, 58, 165
accusations, against political prisoners, 28, 48, 106
Acosta, Luis, 139, 140, 147, 151
Actis, Munú, 21, 49–50, 106, 111
"adaptation," in concentration camps, 21, 71, 92, 104
agency, 20–21
aging, 21, 69, 110, 155
Agostí, Orlando Ramón, 9
"Agustín," 142
Alcázar, Fidel Antonio, 85, 101, 133
Aldini, Cristina, 50
Alessandri, Carlos, 157
Alfonsín, Raul, 24, 26, 42, 153
Alta Gracia, 135
alterations, to buildings, 57–58, 62–63
Álvarez, Juan Carlos, 28, 30, 62, 64–67, 69, 79, 94, 105–106, 148, 150
ambassador, Spanish, 105
amnesia, reactive, 83
Amnesty International, 88
Anti-Communist Alliance Argentina. See Triple A
apolitical, 30, 43, 155
Aranguren de Scheurer, Maria Mercedes "Chicha," 79–80, 163
Archivo. See Comisión y Archivo Provincial de la Memoria de Córdoba
Argañaraz, Jorge L. "Caballo," 129–130
Argente, Hugo, 32–33
Argente, Julio Daniel, 32
Argentine National Commission on the Disappeared (CONADEP), 24, 81, 166
Argentine Revolution, 7
armed leftist movements, 3, 7, 26–27, 44, 46, 66, 70, 154, 166–167
Arrostito, Norma, 59
Aspitia, Américo, 71, 83–84, 85, 116–117, 137–139
Association of Ex-Detainees and Desaparecidos (AEDD), 30, 32, 70

Association of Ex-Presos Políticos de Córdoba (AEPPC): history, 3, 31, 37–39, 41–43, 146, 156–159; identity 4–5, 15, 17, 21, 46, 51, 72, 118, 140; meetings 28–30, 51–53; projects, 20, 45, 51, 61, 70, 74, 76, 86, 109; public perceptions, 23, 33, 45, 148; president, 5, 37, 71, 158
attic, in ESMA, 58

Basso, Atilio, 29, 71, 86, 140, 147, 149
Basso, Hugo, 137–138
Battle of the Panties, 14–15, 99, 103
bifurcated identity, 86
biodanza (dance of life), 133, 164n3
black humor, 73
blacklisting, 130
blood tie, 29
blood money, 153
Bonafini, Hebe de, 32, 55, 153
Bonasso, Miguel, 46
bonds, state, 25, 142–143, 152–153
Borer, Tristan Anne, 45
brain damage, from torture, 80
breaking under torture, 30, 45, 48, 50
broken partnerships, 110, 117–130
Buen Pastor, 112
Buenos Aires: capital, 16–17, 19, 21, 30–31, 32, 34–35, 62, 70; headquarters, 5, 10, 165; province, 6, 12, 96, 112, 121, 158, 168
bureaucracy, 22, 129

Cabildo, 34, 62–63, 126, 161
Cabral, Ester, 84, 95–98, 117
Calviero, Pilar, 32
Cámpora, Héctor, 8, 113
Campos Clandestinos de Detención (CCDs), 53, 126, 145
Cannizzo, Sebastián, 37, 150
cárcel común (regular prison), 9, 13, 51, 53, 75, 78, 90, 98–103
carmelo (hard candy), 15, 162n9
Carter, Jimmy, 14
Casa Rosada, 11
Casino de Oficiales, 55

Catela da Silva, Ludmila, 2, 28, 63
Catholic Church: conservative, 62; progressive wing of, 4, 98, 101.
celda de castigo (punishment cell), 102–103
Center for Legal and Social Studies (CELS), 19, 32
certificate of good conduct, 132–133, 135–136
Chaco, 94, 97
Chamorro, Rubén Jacinto, 59
children, of prisoners, 49, 75, 83–84, 91–92, 96–97, 111–112, 126, 139
Christian Institute of Social Study and Political Action, 111
"civil death," 20
clandestine, living, 41, 164n1
Clara, Mirta, 106
Clarín (newspaper), 32
cold showers, as torture, 81–82
cold temperature, as torture, 82
Cold War, 27
collaborator, 30, 45, 48–54, 65, 69–70, 78
collective identity, 90–92
collective memory, 20, 133
collective, of political prisoners, 3, 32, 162n10
collective punishment, 15, 93
collective struggle, 27, 46, 67
Comisión y Archivo Provincial de la Memoria de Córdoba: creation of, 39–41; fieldsite, 18, 34–37, 61, 118, 122, 126, 130, 147, memorialized space, 51, 54; 64–65, 67.
commemoration, 31–32, 65, 157
committed, to the revolutionary cause, 50
Commission of Families of Political Detainees, 10
Communist Party, 7, 98, 126, 134, 136
community-building, 90–95
communal ties, in society, 27
compañero/a (comrade): AEPPC members, 30, 34, 37, 41, 42–43, 52, 67, 87, 123; cellmates, 89–91, 93–96, 98, 100–101, 106, 120; comrades in Córdoba, 38, 86; definition, 162n8; disappeared comrades, 35, 45, 46, 53, 69–70, 78, 83, 86, 151; survivors, 48–49, 51, 118, 128, 140
Concejo de Guerra (War Council), 15
concentration camps: description, 1, 11–14, 50–51, 74; experiences, 90, 97, 104; ESMA, 61; Holocaust, 21, 100, 102; La Perla, 48; pilot, 9, 157; trauma, 73
conflict, internal with other human rights groups, 28–29
coping strategies, 90, 99, 103–104
Córdoba: CCDs, 9, 51, 61, 74; census, 128, 140; description, 6, 7, 31, 34–36, 53, 63, 89, 145; leftist activity, 15, 25, 37, 149; location, 4, 32–33, 18, 42, 80; repression, 10–11, 13, 27, 29, 66, 158; trial, 39, 48, 151
Cordobazo, 7, 64, 124

Correa, Cristina, 137
counterrevolutionary human rights, 27
coup of March 24, 1976, 31, 65, 94, 114, 156–157
crimes against humanity, 85
cuarteto (type of folk music), 89
"Cynthia," 73, 163n1

D2: CCD, 11–12, 77–78; archive, 11, 18, 34, 51, 102; tour, 56, 61–70, 74
D'Ambra, Nona, 39, 126–128
Damonte, Luis Jorge, 141
"damned," 48
"Daniel," 48
Das, Veena, 110, 143
death as a means of social change, 69
death, early, 140
death flights, 54, 56, 58, 65
death squads, 11, 115
decision-making, among political prisoners in Córdoba, 51
defeat, of youth movements, 55, 67
dehumanization, 47, 56, 57, 81
degrading prison conditions, 72, 80, 109, 146
democracy, 7, 68, 105, 127, 147, 161n3
demonization, 43
denial, 83–84, 87,
dental care, as torture, 56, 82
"depoliticize," 27
depression, 72, 85, 103, 121
desaparecido (disappeared), 1, 4; fallen comrades, 25, 27, 31, 41, 69, 126–127, 145; official victims, 24, 42, 45, 47–48, 128, 146, 154
detention centers, 19, 34, 88, 158, 165, 167
Deutsch, Ana, 85
Díaz, Florencio, 6–10, 15–17
Díaz, María Cristina, 6, 8–17
dichotomy, between hero and traitor, 47
dictatorship, 1, 9, 11–12; before, 158
Diez, Rolo, 46
dirty war, 1
disappear: definition, 161n1; general tactic, 26, 29, 41, 57, 66, 68–69, 95, 139; specific cases, 35, 39, 46, 48, 79–80, 115, 119
discrimination, 128–130, 147–148, 157
distribution, of wealth, 150
Doctrine of National Security, 9
dual presence, at memorialized spaces, 46
Due Obedience law, 24, 26
Duhalde, Luis, 36, 163n5

economic collapse, 25, 143
economic models, 66, 68
education, subversive, 99–102; public, 152
"effective historical reparation," 35
effects, of state terrorism, 108–109, 140
Eichenberger, Élida "Ely," 42, 48, 83, 93–94, 102–104, 106, 134–136

elections, in the AEPPC, 156
elites, as collaborators, 57, 66, 110
empanadas (meat pies), 35
Enclausados, 112–113
era of impunity, 25
ERP (People's Revolutionary Army), 7
escape, 10, 77, 95–96, 112, 114–116
escraches (staged protests), 25
Eslabones (book) 18, 76
ESMA: CCD, 150; memorialized space, 31;
   testimony, 21, 49, 50, 106, 111; tour, 54–
   65, 68–70
Etchecolatz, Miguel, 35
evaluation, of transitional justice in Argentina, 148–153
execution: mock, 93, 120; political, 15, 135
exile, political, 57
Ex Presos Políticos por la Patria Grande,
   159
Ezieza International Airport massacre, 8

failure, of the revolutionary dream, 47
"falling" (into the hands of the military),
   50
Falkland Islands, 24
false documents, 125
Familiares (Families of the Disappeared
   and Those Imprisoned for Political Reasons): archive activity, 37; Buenos Aires,
   32, 60; Córdoba, 33–34, 36, 39–41, 77,
   80; history, 10; relationship with AEPPC,
   29, 38
family strain, 136–139
Faulk, Karen Ann, 2
Federal Tribunal Building, 48
Feitlowitz, Marguerite, 2, 9
Ferrandans, Hugo, "Gato," 143
Ferraro, Víctor Eduardo, 140
Ferreyra, Ovidio Ramón "Pajarito," 81, 129
fieldwork, 18–19, 34–38, 147
figure, of the desaparecido, 128
film, as social threat, 99, 134
film projects, 18, 72, 133, 136, 162n10
financial need, among political prisoners
   in Córdoba, 52
"fishbowl," 59
food, in prison, 81–82
Franco, Francisco, 105
Frankl, Victor, 102
Fresnada, Martín, 39, 163n5

Gaetán, Pedro Nolasco, 98–99
Gardella, Liliana, 50
"Gentleman's Coup," 9
grandchildren, missing, 11, 58, 164n6, 165
gray zone, 45–46, 47–48, 69, 146, 154
grief, parental, 137
"grill," for torture, 75
group therapy, 73
grupo de tareas (task groups), 11

guerrillas, 23, 26–27, 42, 44
Guembe, Maria José, 142
Guest, Iain, 87
Guevara, Che, 78
guilt, 3, 16, 26, 28, 106, 121, 137, 153
"guilty victims," 44, 61, 69, 116, 145

"hair salon," 92
Hagelin, Dagmar, 46
handcuffs, 11–12, 14, 57, 96
health census, 35, 52, 140, 149
heart failure, 86
Heker, Liliana, 46
heroes, desaparecidos as, 47
hiding, 21
HIJOS (Hijos por la Identidad y la Justicia y
   contra el Olivido y el Silencio): branch
   in Córdoba, 33–34, 37, 39–41; history,
   25, 29
history, as told in memorialized spaces,
   64, 147
Holocaust, 21, 100
homemakers, 102
"hooded," 49, 57, 97
human rights, 5, 148
humanity, keeping a sense of, 80, 100

IMF (International Monetary Fund), 25
impunity, 1–2, 25, 149, 151, 153, 167
indigenous people, 63, 86
individualism, 28
innocence, 26, 44, 60–61, 154
inspections, forced bodily, 15, 98–99, 103,
   162n9
inspections, by international human rights
   groups, 12–13, 61, 92
intellectuals, 4, 7, 59, 67, 99–100, 102, 122
intelligence, 11, 34, 57, 77, 114–115, 165–166
internal exile, 9, 110, 111, 116–117, 164
intervention, by international human
   rights actors, 13
interrogation, 11, 57, 61, 65, 74–75, 79, 90,
   96, 119–120
Interpol, 113
irrecuperable (unable to be rehabilitated), 135
isolation, 12, 91–94, 102

Jelin, Elizabeth, 1, 27–28, 45
Jesuits, 34, 63
job discrimination, 128–136
"justice cascade," 148
justice, trials, 151

kidnapping, 119
kinship ties, 2, 5, 24, 27–29, 30, 39, 41–42,
   45, 161n5
Kirchner, Néstor, 26, 43, 148–151
Kirchner, Cristina Fernández de, 26, 148–
   151, 163n5
"Kirchners, los," 148

labor history, 4, 7
labor unions, 17, 36, 40; activism and, 7, 67, 116, 130–132; belonging to, 4, 19, 28, 29, 42, 46, 79, 129, 137; leaders of, 63, 114
Lanusse, Alejandro, 8
La Plata, 25, 121–122, 125, 161n7, 167–168
Lastiri, Rául Alberto, 8
Law 9286 (archive), 37
Law 20508 (amnesty), 8
Law 24043 (indemnity), 142
Law 24411 (reparation to families of the disappeared), 153
laws, impunity, 25–26, 149
Leebaw, Bronwyn Anne, 27
Ledesma, Judge Adolfo Zamboni, 15
Levi, Primo, 21, 47, 146
Levingston, Roberto, 7–8
Lewin, Miriam, 50
libertad vigilada (supervised release), 16, 103, 135–136
library, of archive in Córdoba, 63, 67, 118
Light and Power Union, 36
limbo, in terms of guilt or innocence, 26
lobbying, 18, 35–36, 38, 72, 74, 143, 145, 158
logistics, 57
Longoni, Ana, 46–48
López, Jorge Julio, 35
loss of identity, 111

Madres de Plaza de Mayo, 2, 11, 24, 27, 29, 31, 41, 150; Association of Madres, 32, 55, 153; Córdoba, 30; definition, 162n1; Founding Line, 54;
Malvinas, 24
Mandela, Nelson, 44
Mandela, Winnie, 44
marginalization, 5, 28, 31, 43, 51, 146, 154
Mariano Moreno, 11
Martínez, María Elba, 140
Martínez, Irene, 34, 37, 136, 137
Martos, Silvia, 149
martyr, desaparecido as, 47
"Marvin," 150–151, 153
Massacre of Margarita Belén, 95
Massera, Emilio Eduardo, 9
mate, 18, 59, 73, 104, 118
McKinney, Kelly, 106–107
measuring success of transitional justice, 155
meetings, of the AEPPC, 4, 18, 28, 36–38, 48, 51–52, 71–73, 118, 156
memorials, 4, 17, 20, 22, 26, 45–46, 88, 151; memorial museums, 5, 51, 53–54, 69, 72, 146
memorialized spaces: in Buenos Aires 31–32, 54–61, 70, 68; in Córdoba, 61–68, 166
Memory Park (Parque de la Memoria), 31–32
memory, traumatic, 84
Mendoza, 158
Menem, Carlos Saúl, 25–27, 142
Menéndez, Luciano Benjamín, 13, 17, 48, 73, 85, 93, 115, 128, 151

"Mengele," 87
mental health care, 102–105
mental illness, 60, 83
methods, 4, 17–18, 36, 38
military rule, 7–8, 24, 79, 129
milk can, in prison, 12, 90, 104
Misiones, 95, 97
Molina, Stella, 35
Montoneros, 7, 28, 59, 76, 98, 134
Moore, Charlie, 78, 163n4
morale, in prison, 91
Morse code, 100
Moyn, Samuel, 27
Municipal Office for Human Rights, 122
myths, about the whereabouts of desaparecidos, 127

narrative, 26, 43, 53, 56, 61, 67–68, 154
National Archive of Memory, 54
National Association of Political Prisoners, 158
National Day for Memory and Justice, 31
National University of Córdoba, 7, 37
neglect of political prisoners, 30
negro, en (under the table), 129, 164n8
neoliberalism, 2, 28
Nieva, Manuel, 62–67, 143
Nixon, Richard, 14
noms de guerre, 21, 30
noncollaboration, 95–99
norm, societal, 148
Noto, Rosa, 71
Novillo, Rodolfo "Petiso," 118–126, 148–149
numbers, given to political prisoners, 56–57, 65
Nunca Más (Never Again), 24, 26, 81, 88

OAS (Organization of American States), 13, 14
Office of Human Rights, 122, 126
oligarchy, 28
Onganía, Juan Carlos, 7, 8, 112
operations, in the military, 56–57, 61, 114–115, 135, 161n4
oral history archive, 19, 38, 42, 72, 75, 86–87, 106, 137, 147
Ortiz, Dianna, 86

packages, military euphemism for subversives, 59
packages, in prison, 91–92
Página 12 (newspaper), 32, 55
"Pamela," 84–85
panic attack, 84–85
paperwork, 130–131
paranoia, 72, 139
pardon, presidential, 26
parilla, la (torture with electric prod), 75
Partido Revolucionario de los Trabajadores (PRT), 7, 28–29, 77–78, 86, 95–96, 118, 123, 126, 134

Pasaje de Santa Catalina, 35, 62, 78
past, denied, 28
PEN (Poder Ejecutivo Nacional), 135
pension, state, 5, 136, 139, 140, 143, 147, 156–158
pension law, 157
Peralta, Norma, 76–78, 88–89, 152–153
Pérez, María del Carmen "Carmencita." 75–76, 80–81, 101
Perla, la (prison camp): CCD, 11, 61–62, 74, 150, 163n2, 164n2; experiences, 76, 79–81, 90, 119–120, 124–125, 127; memorialized space, 18, 36, 51–53; 2008 trial, 48, 49
Perón, Eva, 6
Perón, Isabel, 8–9, 114, 134
Perón, Juan Domingo, 6–8, 123
peronismo, 6
Peronist Party, 6–9, 98, 111–112, 114, 134
Peronist Youth, 79
perpetrators of genocide, 46, 53, 153–154
personería jurídica (legal status), 38–39
phases, of public perceptions toward political prisoners, 23, 42
phrases, popular, 28, 146,
picana, la, (electric prod), 74–76
Plaza de Mayo, 2, 31
Plaza de San Martín, 34
police brutality, 2, 7, 16–17, 44, 74, 78
police collaboration, 65, 93, 113–114, 161n4
police officer, notable, 35, 114–115
police stations, former, 11, 34, 62, 76, 123, 135, 165–166
police surveillance, 66, 133
política (politics), 52
political: change, 138; commitment, 26, 40, 52, 70, 77, 87, 126, 162n8; dissidents, 25, 40, 63, 74, 129; movements, 27, 61, 64, 89, 98, 124; organizations, 29, 97; opposition, 7, 146; prisoners, 1–6, 20, 28, 32; violence, 9
political prisoner: in Córdoba 141, 143, 159; definition, 48–49, 51, 53–54; experiences, 50–51, 73, 116, 137, 139; marginalization, 42, 45, 128–130
Ponze, Paty, "Ponze," 134
pos-trauma (post-traumatic stress disorder, PTSD), 72
post-transitional justice, 6, 145, 148, 153–155
"pregnancy wing," 58
pregnant, 11, 74, 97, 115, 123
priests, Catholic, 57, 88
print media, 24, 55, 60, 96
Process for National Reorganization, 9
Program for Torture Victims, 85
Project Condor, 114
Provincial Conference for Former Political Prisoners, 42
Pujadas, las, 134

psychologists, 71, 84
psychological effects of torture, 14, 22, 72, 79–80, 83, 86, 97, 140
psychological torture methods, 51, 75, 90, 102–103
public appearances, in schools, 40, 61, 63, 67, 88
pueblo (the people), 64, 109
punishment cell, 102–103, 113
Punto Final law, 26

quebrado (broken), 71, 87, 98

radio, 97, 117
rape, in prison, 73, 163n1
Rawson prison, 112
"reappeared," 54, 68, 111, 146
recuperable (able to be rehabilitated), 135
Rega, José López, 8
Regalado, Gladys, 28, 35, 100, 104–105, 118–126, 149
regular prisoners, 12, 96
reintegration, social, 116
reintegration, into family life, 113–114
release, from prison, 16–17, 79, 85, 98, 102, 105, 121, 131
reparation: first indemnity 142–143, second set of reparations, 144, 156–158
reparation, for families of the disappeared, 25; rejection of, 152–153, 158
resistance, 21, 90–92, 95, 100–101, 106
Resistencia prison, 94
resolution, creating the Archivo, 41
retirement, 129, 133, 136, 143, 157
revolution, 5, 27–28, 47, 69, 154
Ribera, la (prison camp), 11, 90, 119–121, 125, 127
Rice, Patrick, 88
Rosario, 111–112, 115, 131

Sacco, Enzo, "Gringo," 130
Saint-Exupéry, Antoine de, 66
Santa Fe, 134
Scalet, Richard, 140
Schreurer, Carlos Enrique, 79–80
Secretariat for Human Rights in Córdoba Province, 36, 109, 129, 149
secret documents, 130
security depository, 142
selection of victims, 58
self-care, 90–92
sensory deprivation, 12–13, 74, 80
separation, family, 138–139
Servicio Paz y Justicia, 37
shackles, 57
Sikkink, Kathryn, 27
silenced, political prisoners, 5, 48, 87, 111, 140, 147, 154
"singing," 50, 98
slogan, "memory, truth, justice," 43, 161n3
social change, 5, 22, 43, 64, 123, 146, 148, 155

socioeconomic impacts, of imprisonment, 109–110
solidarity: memories, 21, 86, 88–92, 95, 99–100, 106; movements, 29; prison experiences, 16, 21, 69, 72, 81; protest, 15; value, 33, 35, 37, 71, 105, 124, 146, 158
Sosa, Mercedes, 66
Sotti, Monica, 88–89
South Africa's Truth and Reconciliation Commission, 44
Spain, 7–8, 105
split, in the AEPPC, 156
Staps, Alicia, 38–41, 108, 111–116, 149
state terrorism: defined , 74, 90; effects of, 108–109, 116, 117, 140–141, 143; reparation, 152, 155, 157; resistance, 139; state blame, 61; victims of, 4–5, 43, 144–145, 147–148
steadfast, activists, 48, 71, 89
stigma, 5, 43, 54, 109–110, 136, 140, 146–147, 157
strategies, while under torture, 83, 96
stolen babies, 25
storytelling, 133
students: as primary targets of military, 8–9, 64, 99, 111, 136; image of desaparecidos, 27; university, 7, 64; who give tours, 55–56, 68; visitors at D2, 63–64, 66–67, 102
student council, 6, 79, 134
submarino, 75
subversives, 9, 66, 96, 99–100, 102, 125, 130, 135, 141
suffering, social, 5, 20, 26, 72, 73, 86, 88, 109, 110, 143
Supreme Court, Argentine, 149
surveillance, state, 25
survivor guilt: blame, 3, 26, 28, 44–45, 61, 69, 116 145; emotion, 16, 106, 121, 137
survivors, 4

taboo, on speaking about the past, 25
task groups, 11
Taylor, Julie, 15
"telephone," the game in prison, 94, 99
terrorists, 9, 14, 26, 42–44, 106, 141, 146, 153
theater, in prison, 93–94
therapy, 71
Third Army Corps, 48, 93, 115
Third World Movement, 111
traitor, 45–48, 54, 69, 106, 145, 153
"transfer," 12, 51, 60, 62, 65, 74, 92, 158, 161n7, 167
transferred, in testimonies, 14, 76, 79, 90, 94, 97, 112–113, 119, 121, 127
translator, informal, for political prisoners, 18, 62

transitional justice: Argentina, 22–24, 26–27, 109, 155; definition, 1–3, 6; limits, 128, 145; survivor views, 42–43, 148–154
Todorov, Tzvetan, 100
Tokar, Elisa, 50
Torres, Sonia, 34
Torriglia, Jorge Alfredo, 151
torture: consequences of, 79, 83–85, 108, 117, 141, 157; experiences in prison, 81; tour theme, 62–70
Torture Abolition and Survivor Support Coalition, 86
tours, 54–70
tour guides, 52–54
transitional justice, 1
Trial of the Junta leaders, 24
Triple A (Argentine Anti-Communist Alliance) 22, 23, 128, 148, 181
truth commission, 1, 20, 44, 85, 88, 145, 151, 166
tweezing, eyebrow, 90–91, 104
Two Demons Theory, 26–27, 42

U9 (Penitentiary Unit Number 9 of La Plata), 121
underground, living, 7–8, 77, 112, 114, 117
United States, 14, 38, 64, 86, 164n1
United States National Security Archive, 14, 19
UP1 (Penitentiary Unit Number 1 of San Martín): defined, 10; experiences, 12–14, 17, 78, 90, 93, 104, 121, 127; film, 18, 133
Uruguay, 114

verdes, los, 126
Vergara, Viviana "Vivi," 82, 90, 99, 130
victim vs. perpetrator, 154
victimhood, 5
victimization: dual, 146; societal, 26
Videla, Jorge Rafael, 9, 17
Villa, Juan, 108, 117
Villa Devoto, 12, 14–16, 92, 112, 121, 127, 135
visitors: at D2, 18, 61–68; at ESMA, 55–57; at La Perla, 36; at memorialized spaces in general, 46, 53–54, 70
violations, against political prisoners, 38

Waitman, Sara Liliana: activism, 39–40; AEPPC president, 5, 32–33, 71, 158; key informant, 35–38; prison experiences, 82, 99, 118, 126–128, 141
"walled up," 57
walls, in former secret detention centers, 58, 63–66
walls, prison, 16, 93. 102, 104, 119–120
water, 75–76, 81–82, 97, 157, 163n2
Western civilization, 9
witnesses, 5, 20, 35, 48–49, 52, 107
work, 129. See also negro, en

ABOUT THE AUTHOR

REBEKAH PARK is a research scholar with the Center for the Study of Women at University of California, Los Angeles, and works as an applied anthropologist in New York City.